BOURBON
is my Comfort Food

BOURBON

is my Comfort Food

THE BOURBON WOMEN® GUIDE TO FANTASTIC COCKTAILS AT HOME

HEATHER WIBBELS

Foreword by Susan Reigler

UNIVERSITY PRESS OF KENTUCKY

Copyright © 2022 by The University Press of Kentucky

Scholarly publisher for the Commonwealth, serving
Bellarmine University, Berea College, Centre College of
Kentucky, Eastern Kentucky University, The Filson His-
torical Society, Georgetown College, Kentucky Historical
Society, Kentucky State University, Morehead State
University, Murray State University, Northern Kentucky
University, Spalding University, Transylvania University,
University of Kentucky, University of Louisville, and
Western Kentucky University.
All rights reserved.

Editorial and Sales Offices:
The University Press of Kentucky
663 South Limestone Street, Lexington, Kentucky
40508-4008
www.kentuckypress.com

Cover and interior design by Jennifer L. Witzke

Cataloging-in-Publication data available
from the Library of Congress

ISBN 978-0-8131-8689-4 (hardcover : alk. paper)
ISBN 978-0-8131-8705-1 (pdf)
ISBN 978-0-8131-8691-7 (epub)

This book is printed on acid-free paper meeting
the requirements of the American National Standard
for Permanence in Paper for Printed Library Materials.

Manufactured in the United States of America.

Member of the Association of University Presses

To my honey, my family, and my best friend:

Thank you for your encouragement over the years and your personal sacrifice in taste-testing your way through hundreds of cocktails.

A toast to all the Bourbon Women
who've inspired me over the years:

Here's to the girls
who love whiskey:
May their laughter be bold,
May their stories never grow old,
And their nights
Be just a little bit frisky.

CONTENTS

FOREWORD

In 2010, my friends Cynthia Torp and Peggy Noe Stevens were working with one of Kentucky's legacy distilleries on a design for a new visitors' center. This was one of many distillery projects in the works as bourbon's renaissance was well under way and bourbon tourism was growing exponentially. During a break in a meeting, Cynthia and Peggy, both bourbon enthusiasts (in fact, Peggy was the world's first female master bourbon taster), looked at each other with recognition. The meeting was all about marketing to men between the ages of twenty-five and fifty-five. Targeting that demographic was standard practice throughout the bourbon industry. But Peggy and Cynthia knew that overlooking women was a mistake. The distillers were neglecting a portion of the consumer population that could greatly expand their market. How could they get the bourbon producers to recognize what they were missing?

That's when the idea for the Bourbon Women Association was born. Peggy and Cynthia organized focus groups and invited some women they knew who enjoyed bourbon to a few bourbon cocktail and hors d'oeuvre receptions. As an established bourbon writer, I was one of those women. Surveys of the attendees revealed that the women were keen to find out more about the history and technology of making bourbon, and they were excited to do so in a supportive atmosphere of inquiry and education. (This was another reason that Peggy had long had an idea about starting such a group.) They also saw it as a great opportunity to connect with other like-minded women.

Peggy and Cynthia were determined to make Bourbon Women not only an educational organization that could provide behind-the-scenes experiences and access to industry experts but also an opportunity to mentor other women who were interested in pursuing careers in the industry. They kept the membership fee low so younger women could join, and from the very first, they wanted to do good through philanthropy, as well as by helping members connect with one another and with people in the larger bourbon community and supporting women already working in the industry.

Heather Wibbels joined Bourbon Women soon after it was formed in 2011. She was not involved in the bourbon industry, but she enjoyed whiskey and discovered she had a passion for creating cocktails. I remember being at a Bourbon Women meeting when she pulled a little bottle out of her purse, along with some tasting cups, and asked if anyone would like to sample her latest creation. We all did.

One of Bourbon Women's annual events is the "Not Your Pink Drink" contest. In the interest of busting stereotypes, one of the rules is that the drink cannot be pink. (Take that, Cosmos!) Heather entered the amateur division and won three years in a row. That's when the group put her in charge of judging the contest.

When I stepped down after several years as chair of the Bourbon Women board of directors, Peggy held a little party for me and asked Heather to bring the cocktails. Heather arrived with two different batched concoctions, both of which were complex, balanced, and, best of all, delicious. That evening, Peggy dubbed her the "Cocktail Contessa."

Today, Heather's *Cocktail Contessa* blog reaches thousands of subscribers. She consults with distilleries to create cocktails tailored to their whiskeys' taste profiles, and she now serves as chair of the Bourbon Women board. She also writes about cocktails for two magazines. She has benefited from her association with Bourbon Women exactly as Peggy and Cynthia envisioned, and she is one among many.

Heather's passion and creativity are on display in *Bourbon Is My Comfort Food.* In addition to her own recipes, she has gathered many from other Bourbon Women members. The group started in Louisville, but it now has hundreds of members across the United States and organized branches in fourteen other cities. (Check out bourbonwomen.org for the locations.) Almost 300 separate events have been hosted by the organization, from tastings with master distillers to hands-on whiskey making. The annual Bourbon Women SIPosium conference draws attendees from more than thirty states.

Today, many more women are visible in the world of bourbon, from distillers and chemists to executives and spokespeople. Many more women have become prominent mixologists. And the activities and visibility of Bourbon Women have raised distilleries' awareness of a group of consumers they no longer neglect.

Cheers to Bourbon Women as it enters its second decade and to Heather Wibbels's book, which celebrates women's enjoyment of America's native spirit.

Susan Reigler

PREFACE

Every journey starts with a single step. My bourbon journey started with a single sip. When I moved back to Kentucky in 2011, I wanted to learn more about the spirit and the industry that are so central to my home. For my fortieth birthday, I planned a Kentucky Bourbon Trail excursion and was hooked. From my first step into a rickhouse, the scent of the angel's share wafting around me, I fell in love. Every tasting and tour expanded my fascination with bourbon.

Shortly thereafter I discovered Bourbon Women. This group of women dedicated to celebrating not just bourbon but also bourbon culture felt like home to me. And I wanted everyone to join me on my whiskey journey. For years I struggled to get anyone other than my best friend to love bourbon as much as I did. Finally, a wayward old-fashioned at the Village Anchor restaurant in Louisville piqued my husband's interest. He took one sip of mine and then ordered his own. The door had opened.

So I learned to make old-fashioneds. I started experimenting with different syrups and bitters. Every Friday night I would make two different recipes and let my husband decide which one he preferred. I then asked him to help me pick out the bourbon beforehand, so he started sipping whiskey neat to discern the best bourbon for his Friday night cocktail. Over a matter of months, he was converted to a neat whiskey drinker. I lost my designated driver, but my bourbon collection expanded exponentially.

In the process of creating cocktails to convert friends and family, I started entering amateur cocktail contests. After winning the Bourbon Women "Not Your Pink Drink" contest for the third year in a row, I was invited to be a judge and to create cocktail content for members. To say that I had found my passion is an understatement.

I am fascinated by the breadth of flavors in bourbon and the process of combining them in thoughtful and elegant ways to make approachable cocktails. It feels more like a calling than work. Teaching others the beauty and brilliance of bourbon cocktails widens bourbon's influence. It invites others to taste and experience what I already love. I want everyone to find joy in mixing a bourbon cocktail.

I joined Bourbon Women's board of directors in 2018, and in late 2020 Susan Reigler and Peggy Noe Stevens came up with the idea of creating a book of cocktails to celebrate the tenth anniversary of the group's founding and to share our love of bourbon cocktails with the world. We wanted to salute winners of our cocktail contests, highlight cocktail recipes representing our growth across the country, and share tips about creating bourbon cocktails with other bourbon enthusiasts.

For many bourbon lovers, a sip of bourbon feels like coming home. It's our comfort food. Whether we work in the industry or sip with friends, the scent of bourbon causes us to take a big breath, close our eyes, and relax into the tasting experience. So why not pour yourself a glass, sit back, and breathe in that beautiful aroma as we talk about bourbon?

Tasting from the barrel in the Jeptha Creed rickhouse.
(Photo by Chris Joyce KY)

INTRODUCTION

Cocktails Are the Gateway to Bourbon

Cocktails are the gateway to bourbon. Many bourbon enthusiasts start their journey with a bourbon cocktail. Handing a bourbon newbie a delectable, balanced, and beautifully presented cocktail makes bourbon approachable. It opens the door to explore what all the fuss (and fun) is about. It's a springboard for the excitement of gathering with a group of friends to chat with whiskey in hand.

For a long time, that conversation was dominated by men. But in 2011 that changed when Peggy Noe Stevens and a small group of passionate women founded Bourbon Women, the first spirits group dedicated to women and their love of bourbon. This was more than a drinking club where women chatted over bourbon cocktails. It was the start of a group that celebrates not just bourbon but bourbon culture throughout the country and around the world.

Ten years later, Bourbon Women has hundreds of members and branches nationwide. The group has hosted hundreds of signature bourbon events and has come to be recognized by consumers and the spirits industry as a leader in connecting bourbon enthusiasts and bourbon companies through great experiences. This book honors and celebrates those ten years of fun, entertainment, and education by sharing a love of bourbon cocktails. However, this book is more than just a compilation of cocktails; it's a primer on the elements of classic bourbon cocktails and how to create your own variations on them. It's a guide to educating your palate to appreciate the combi-

The Founder's Manhattan

This Black Manhattan has just enough amaro to deepen the flavors and round out the sweetness of a great bourbon. Amaro's bittersweet flavor adds both earthiness and herbal sweetness to the cocktail to replace the usual sweet vermouth. The orange bitters and cherry juice are a nod to the traditional garnishes for a classic Manhattan cocktail—a high-quality cocktail cherry or an expressed orange peel.

---

2 ounces bourbon

¼ teaspoon Luxardo cherry juice

2 dashes orange bitters

Splash of amaro (just enough to change the color)

Garnish: Luxardo cherry

Combine bourbon, cherry juice, bitters, and amaro in a mixing glass, add ice, and stir until well chilled, about 30 seconds. Strain into a chilled glass and garnish.

By Peggy Noe Stevens, founder of Bourbon Women

Bourbon ready for tasting.

spend more time tasting and nosing whiskeys and cocktails. And who doesn't love an excuse to sip more whiskey?

Whether you are new to bourbon or already steeped in its history and lifestyle, this book gives you the tools to make great bourbon cocktails, share them with friends and family, and expand your whiskey circles—because the only thing better than a bourbon cocktail is enjoying it with others. Let's start with some bourbon basics.

What Is Bourbon?

Like any whiskey, bourbon must be made from grains and aged in an oak container. But to be called bourbon, a spirit must meet specific legal requirements. A law passed by Congress in 1964 designated bourbon "a distinctive product of the United States" and set the following rules:

- Bourbon can be made only in the United States (but it can be made in any state).

- Bourbon must be at least 51 percent corn by mash bill (recipe).

- Bourbon must be distilled at 160 proof or below.

- Bourbon must go into the barrel at 125 proof or below.

- Bourbon must be aged in a new charred oak container (it doesn't have to be a barrel).

- Bourbon cannot contain any additives or substances other than water (no coloring or flavoring agents can be added).

BOURBON TRIVIA

Not included on the list of regulations is how long bourbon must be aged. There is no minimum age, but to be called *straight bourbon,* it must be aged at least two years. And if straight bourbon is aged less than four years, the label must designate how long the bourbon has been aged. So if a label says "straight bourbon whiskey" and doesn't list an age, you can bet it's at least four years old.

nation of bourbon and other flavor elements and training your senses to seek out flavors that work well with whiskey.

Because of the many variations in the tastes and styles of bourbon whiskey, building cocktails with this spirit is an entertaining exercise in matching flavors and aromas. Harmonizing the underlying flavors of a whiskey with compatible spirits and liqueurs just means that you

These are the guiding principles of all bourbon production, yet they can result in a fascinating breadth and complexity of styles and flavors. Bourbon often has notes of vanilla and caramel, but you may also find hints of nuts, flowers, fruits, citrus, grass, oak, leather, and tobacco. That variety of flavors and aromas makes bourbon a perfect ingredient for cocktails, from the simple whiskey sour to the most complex layered cocktail.

Why Bourbon Works in Cocktails

Many bourbon lovers drink it neat, but bourbon's flavors combine in glorious ways with liqueurs, juices, and syrups. Bourbon can punch through other flavors and add complexity to an otherwise one-note cocktail—especially if you choose a mid- to high-proof spirit.

In Kentucky, we have a saying about bourbon: Enjoy it any way you like. Each bourbon enthusiast has favorites based on aroma, flavor, mouthfeel, and finish. On your bourbon journey, you will learn that you don't have the same preferences and palate as everyone else in the room, but that's the beauty of bourbon and the sensory experience.

Just as bourbon preferences differ, so do cocktail preferences. Some enjoy a sweet cocktail, while others like something more bitter. Keep in mind that the recipes in this book are suggestions, not edicts written in stone. For each of us, the *perfect* cocktail will be different. One person might prefer orange bitters in an old-fashioned with a brown sugar simple syrup. Another might prefer demerara syrup and Angostura bitters.

For the major cocktail categories, I include cocktail "lab experiments" to try at home to develop your palate and discover how elements of the cocktail work together to create the drinking experience. These exercises develop the senses (both smell and taste) in the same way that tasting flights and food pairings do. They will help you determine whether you prefer sweet or bitter cocktails and what spirit-to-modifier ratio appeals to you. They will teach you how to drink cocktails thoughtfully.

In addition to my own cocktail recipes and cocktail labs, I have included recipes developed by the Bourbon Women "Not Your Pink Drink" contest winners (see chapter 12), Bourbon Women branches across the country (see chapter 13), and the group's leadership team. I believe every bourbon enthusiast has a few great cocktails in her.

Cocktails Are Meant to Be Experienced, Not Consumed

Head into a fancy craft cocktail bar or speakeasy and your senses will be astounded by the variety of tastes, colors, and presentations. Mixologists and foodies like to say that you drink and eat with your eyes first, your nose second,

WHISKEY TRIVIA

How does bourbon differ from Scotch whisky and Irish whiskey? All three must be made of grains and produced and aged in their country of origin: the United States, Scotland, and Ireland, respectively. Scotch whisky is made from malted barley, although it can contain other cereal grains; it must use natural enzymes from the malted barley produced through sugar conversion and must be aged at least three years. Irish whiskey, also made of cereal grains, undergoes yeast fermentation like bourbon but has a different maximum distillation proof: 189.6. It also has a three-year minimum age. There are numerous other categories and regulations, but these are the basics.

TIP FROM BOURBON WOMEN

Your palate is your own, in cocktails as in bourbon. Have fun developing your palate to better evaluate cocktails, just as you do bourbon.

Perfect Manhattan
(see chapter 5).

TIP FOR SERVING COCKTAILS AT HOME

For my cocktail photos, I often garnish with bright, colorful, complicated elements to add visual pizzazz. But at home, I use something simple—a swath of citrus, a lightly rimmed glass, or a dusting of spice on the surface. These simple additions add aromatic and flavor components to make a great bourbon cocktail.

and your mouth third. Creating a fabulous cocktail means choosing a great glass (and taking the time to chill or heat it, as appropriate), filling that glass with an amazing concoction, and adding a striking garnish. Every sense should be engaged with each sip.

Remember that anticipation drives the pleasure derived from an experience. If you wait all week before opening a new bottle of bourbon for a special occasion, you're building anticipation. By handing your guest a cocktail with an elegant garnish, you're inviting her to pause and appreciate the experience she's about to enjoy. You're encouraging your guest to stop a moment, take in the cocktail, and linger over it. Anticipation sells a cocktail, and it is seen before it is tasted.

Are you ready to get started? First, you'll need to know the basics of making bourbon and whiskey cocktails at home, including the right tools, whiskeys, bitters, liqueurs, and syrups.

Toasting with bourbon at a Bourbon Women event. (Photo by Chris Joyce KY)

1 | BOURBON BAR BASICS

Mix at Home Like a Pro

Vanilla Old-Fashioned

This old-fashioned includes a vanilla simple syrup made with bourbon-smoked sugar from Bourbon Barrel Foods. The addition of a barrel-aged vanilla and chocolate bitters balances things out. By choosing a bourbon with great vanilla, chocolate, and orange notes, you'll highlight and enhance the whiskey's inherent flavors.

2 ounces Kentucky bourbon

¼ ounce vanilla simple syrup (recipe follows)

1 dash chocolate bitters

Garnish: orange peel

Combine ingredients in a mixing beaker over ice and stir until well chilled. Serve over a single large ice cube in a rocks glass and garnish with a twist of orange peel.

Vanilla Simple Syrup

1 cup water

1 cup Bourbon Barrel Foods bourbon-smoked sugar

1 tablespoon Bourbon Barrel Foods barrel-aged Madagascar vanilla extract

Bring water and bourbon-smoked sugar to a boil. Allow to cool and add vanilla extract. Store in the fridge.

By Susan Reigler, president of Bourbon Women, 2015–2017

We bourbon enthusiasts love to entice our friends and neighbors to join us in the enjoyment of bourbon. Whipping out a long-handled bar spoon and mixing glass to make an old-fashioned or a Manhattan looks impressive and encourages them to ask questions, which in turn lets us teach them about cocktails and bourbon. Sometimes the only thing standing between a bourbon newbie and a passionate bourbon drinker is a little instruction in a fun environment, and a great cocktail can smooth the path.

You can mix bourbon cocktails at home with just a mason jar, a stirrer, and a strainer of some sort, but having the right equipment makes it easier and more fun to create cocktails with consistency. It's tempting to fall down the rabbit hole of cocktail mixology and acquire too many "necessary" tools (you should see how many shakers and bar spoons I've collected), but at its most basic, you need just three things (described in more detail later):

1. Boston cocktail shaker
2. Long-handled bar spoon
3. Hawthorne strainer

Anything else you need already resides in your kitchen. A paring knife, peeler, small cutting board, and hand juicer can easily be recruited for double duty when making whiskey cocktails. Although mixing glasses, muddlers, and electric juicers are nice to have, they're not required; start with the three basics, and add more items when you're ready.

SHOPPING TIP

When purchasing a Hawthorne strainer, look for one with a relatively short handle and a very tight coil. The tighter the coil, the better the strainer will be at filtering out juice pulp, muddled fruit, herb pieces, and ice shards.

Bar Tools for the Home Bourbon Mixologist

COCKTAIL SHAKER

The most basic, must-have piece of equipment is a cocktail shaker. With it, you can make both stirred and shaken cocktails. There are two common types of shakers.

Boston shaker. The staple of bartenders around the world, the Boston shaker consists of a set of two metal tins or one glass tumbler and one metal tin. The best Boston shaker sets have a weighted base to keep the shaking tin upright when you're pouring the ingredients in, muddling, or fitting on a strainer.

Cobbler shaker. This three-piece shaker includes a mixing glass, a top with a built-in strainer, and a cap. This type of shaker is easy for beginners to use because it doesn't require an extra strainer. Make sure to wrap a finger or thumb over the cap to keep it secure and to keep the cocktail in the shaker as you shake.

BAR SPOON

The perfect bar spoon has a long handle with a twisted spiral stem and a small, shallow bowl. The best bar spoons are weighted at the end to ensure balance and a smooth motion while stirring. The twisted spiral handle enables you to twist the spoon with a flick of the fingers, letting it glide along the inside of the mixing glass.

STRAINER

There are two main types of strainers.

Hawthorne strainer. The Hawthorne strainer is a flat, paddle-shaped strainer with an attached coil and a small handle. It is used primarily with a Boston shaker. The strainer fits, coil side down, into the cocktail shaker.

Julep strainer. The julep strainer looks like a large, shallow slotted spoon. It fits perfectly in the bowl of a mixing glass.

Hawthorne strainer

Julep strainer

Shaker sets, strainers, jiggers, bar spoons, and other barware.

Boston shaker

Mixing glass

Muddler

Bar spoon

Metal sieve

Highball glass

Champagne flute

Toddy mug

Julep cup

Coupe

Rocks glass

Copper mule mug

Julep cup, highball glass, champagne flute,
toddy mug, rocks glass, coupe, and mule mug.

HANDHELD JUICER

A handheld juicer is essential for any cocktail requiring citrus juice.

MIXING GLASS

Once I had fallen in love with bourbon cocktails, my first bar tool purchase was a mixing glass and a bar spoon. Mixing glasses (sometimes called mixing beakers) are short pitchers with straight sides and a wide, sturdy base to hold the ingredients and ice cubes while leaving enough room for the bar spoon to glide around the interior. There's nothing like the music of a spoon in a mixing glass as you concoct old-fashioneds or Manhattans. And watching that amber cocktail chill and dilute in the glass is magical.

MUDDLER

The muddler may not be an engineering marvel, but it's a workhorse when making whiskey smashes, jam cocktails, juleps, and more. Consisting of a small wooden or metal cylinder, the muddler acts like a pestle to agitate herbs and grind spices and sugar in the cocktail shaker. If you don't have a muddler, the handle of a wooden spoon is an acceptable alternative.

METAL SIEVE

A small, fine metal sieve with a long handle can be used as a secondary method of straining cocktails. If you love whiskey sours and smashes and prefer them clear rather than cloudy, invest in one.

JULEP TEST

If you don't believe that the cup makes a difference, fix two juleps. Put one in a glass and the other in a metal julep cup. The combination of the metal, ice, and alcohol means that you don't get condensation on the outside of the cup; you get frost. It's a full sensory experience from the frost to the scent of the bourbon to the tickle of the mint garnish.

SHOPPING TIP

Haunt thrift stores and consignment shops to find unusual vintage glassware, which often has beautiful etching, hand-painted designs, or intricate crystal patterns. I love discovering unique glassware, and I don't feel too terrible when I break a glass that cost less than $2.

Glassware for the Home Bourbon Mixologist

I love an elegant cocktail in a beautiful glass, but bourbon cocktails don't require hundreds of different kinds of glasses. Most bourbon cocktails can be enjoyed with just four types of glasses. Your first purchase should be rocks glasses; in a pinch, they can be used for most drinks.

MUST-HAVE GLASSWARE

Rocks (aka old-fashioned or lowball) glass. The best rocks glasses feel solid in the hand and have a heavy base so that you can muddle right in the glass. They come in two sizes: regular (6–10 ounces) and double (12–16 ounces). These are the best starter glasses for a home bar, and if you're a bourbon fan, you probably already have a set.

Coupe glass. This 5- to 7-ounce saucer-shaped, stemmed glass is perfect for a cocktail served up. Originally designed for sipping champagne, the coupe glass can double for Manhattans and champagne cocktails.

Highball glass. These tall, skinny glasses are perfect for cocktails with soda or crushed ice or whenever you want to highlight a fun color gradient. They are similar to a Collins glass but lower in volume (usually 8–12 ounces).

Julep cup. To look like a professional, always serve a julep in a metal julep cup. A highlight of the experience is the frosty metal cup that's almost too cold to hold. No substitute does a julep justice.

Champagne flute. A champagne flute with trails of bubbles floating upward is a beautiful and classy way to serve bourbon brunch cocktails.

Collins glass. This large glass (12–16 ounces) may be too big for a traditional highball but perfect for refreshing, icy, lower-proof summer cocktails such as bourbon lemonade or iced tea.

Copper mule mug. If you're a fan of the mule, purchase a couple of copper mule mugs for bourbon Kentucky mules.

Heatproof glass mug. Although you can serve hot cocktails such as a hot toddy in a ceramic mug, use a glass mug to enjoy the beautiful amber color.

PROFESSIONAL TIP

The order in which ingredients are added to the mixing glass or shaker can be critical, especially if you make a mistake. Bartenders add the most expensive ingredients—the spirits—last. If you follow this practice at home, you can save your whiskey collection from costly cocktail mistakes!

Bar Techniques to Master

Bar techniques may look complicated and impossible to master, but you can find videos on the internet to teach you how to do anything. So if you're having trouble using a long-handled bar spoon in a mixing glass, help is only a click away.

STIRRING

There is nothing more alluring than an amber-colored cocktail swirling around an ice cube in a crystal mixing glass. Just thinking about it makes me sigh in anticipation. With a proper stirring technique, the outside bowl of the spoon circles the inside of the glass, swirling the ice and cocktail together with a soft, lovely sound that announces the start of cocktail hour.

You can use a mason jar and a long-handled spoon to stir a cocktail at home, but I advise investing in a mixing glass and a bar spoon. They make stirring a cocktail effortless, and they're part of the fun and ritual of cocktail creation. Whiskey nerds already love the sound of the cork popping out of a bourbon bottle; with a bar spoon and a little practice, you'll come to love the music of the bar spoon swirling in the glass.

Practice stirring with ice and liquid in the mixing glass, following these three steps:

1. Place the bar spoon in the mixing glass with the outside of the spoon's bowl against the inside of the mixing glass. As you stir, keep the outside of the spoon in contact with the inside of the glass once things get moving.

2. Hold the long handle of the bar spoon vertically between the second and third fingers with your hand thumb up, like reaching out to shake someone's hand. The thumb should rest lightly on the handle of the spoon. (See the photo on the facing page.)

3. Gently pull your fingers toward you and away from you. Each motion rotates the stem of the spoon, pulling it along the inside of the mixing glass.

Once you have mastered this technique, you'll look like an expert behind the bar.

SHAKING

Shaking cocktails looks sexy, and best of all, the technique is less daunting than stirring. With bourbon cocktails, you'll likely be stirring more than shaking, but for cocktails that require juice, like a sour or a smash, or cocktails that contain cream, like a bourbon milk punch or a bourbon fizz, break out your cocktail shaker.

Up refers to a cocktail served chilled, usually in a coupe or martini glass.

Stirring a cocktail in a mixing glass.

The basics are the same whether you use a two-piece or three-piece shaker:

- Verify that all pieces of the shaker are securely fitted so you don't spray the cocktail all over the room.

- Keep a hand on both the top and bottom pieces of the shaker when using a Boston shaker and on the tumbler and cap of a cobbler shaker.

- Use a few larger ice cubes—ideally, 1-inch cubes—rather than pebble or refrigerator ice. They hold their shape better and don't break into chips and shards, which can overdilute the cocktail.

- Hold the shaker horizontally when shaking, and imagine the ice cubes are pistons driving through the cocktail ingredients to chill and aerate them.

- Shake vigorously, like you mean it. It should sound loud next to your ear.

- Limit shaking to 10 to 12 seconds to properly chill and combine the cocktail. It's thoroughly chilled when the outside of the shaker is frosty and painful to hold.

Using a two-piece shaker. The beauty of this kind of cocktail shaker is that the cold temperature of the ice creates a seal that keeps the two parts together while you shake. For the Boston shaker, place the ingredients in the glass tumbler. For an all-metal shaker set, place the ingredients in the smaller tin. Follow these steps:

1. Add the ingredients to the appropriate tin.

2. Fill the other tin with ice, and pour the cocktail ingredients over the ice. Tap down lightly to seal the two pieces. Make sure they are sealed together at a slight angle, not centered. This makes it easier to get them apart once you're done shaking.

3. Hold the shaker horizontally, with one hand on each piece.

4. Shake vigorously, back and forth, for 10 to 12 seconds. You want to drive the ice from one end of the shaker to the other, not wash it back and forth like a lazy lava lamp.

5. Place the shaker on the counter and tap your wrist smartly against the side at the 3 or 9 o'clock position (12 o'clock being the spot where the two tumblers are in closest contact as you look down from above; see the photo on facing page). Pull the top shaking tin off.

6. Fit a Hawthorne strainer on the top of the tin and strain the liquid into a cocktail glass.

Using a three-piece shaker. The process is even simpler when using a three-piece cobbler shaker. Follow these steps:

1. Put the cocktail ingredients in the tumbler and fill with ice.

2. Place the top on the tumbler and make sure the cap covering the strainer is secure.

3. Take hold of the cobbler shaker with one hand on the base. With the fingers or palm of the other hand, hold the cap down.

4. Shake vigorously, horizontally, for 10 to 12 seconds. Drive the ice from the bot-

12

9

3

6

PROFESSIONAL TIP

Be generous with the ice.
Fill the shaker up.

The "clock" on a shaking tin.
To release the seal, strike the
shaker on the side at either 3
or 9 o'clock.

tom of the tin to the cap so that it hits both ends of the shaker.

5. Place the shaker on the bar and remove the cap to reveal the strainer.

6. Pour the cocktail into a prepared glass.

MUDDLING

Muddling just means crushing herbs, spices, or fruit for use in a cocktail. The muddler should be long enough to allow you to hold it comfortably above the rim of the tumbler while in use. Follow these steps:

1. Place the items to be muddled in the bottom of a mixing tin or glass.

2. Add the syrup or sweetening liqueur.

3. Using the muddler, press down against the herbs, spices, or fruit, twisting slightly. This twisting motion rubs pieces of the muddled items against one another, releasing their flavors and aromatics.

Straining with a julep strainer.

PROFESSIONAL TIP

Don't macerate when you muddle. Overmuddling fresh, delicate herbs like mint or basil makes them bitter and leaves pieces floating in the cocktail. When muddling both herbs and fruit for a cocktail such as a peach-basil smash, muddle the peach first; then add the basil and muddle again very lightly. This allows plenty of the peach flavor to be released without overmuddling the basil.

STRAINING

Whether using a Hawthorne strainer or a julep strainer's slotted spoon, the technique is simple. For a Hawthorne strainer, place it coil side down on top of the shaker tumbler filled with

Straining with a Hawthorne strainer.

To double-strain a cocktail, use both a Hawthorne strainer and a fine metal sieve as you pour it into the glass.

PROFESSIONAL TIP

Lightly shake or tap the side of the sieve with the cocktail shaker to keep the liquid moving through the sieve.

ice and cocktail. Use your first finger to hold the strainer tight against the top of the tumbler as you pour the cocktail into a glass.

For a julep strainer, place the bowl of the strainer spoon in the mixing glass so that it holds back the ice. Use your first finger to press down on the handle of the spoon while pouring the cocktail into the glass.

DOUBLE STRAINING

With this method, the cocktail passes through a Hawthorne strainer and then a metal sieve as it's poured into the glass. Double straining is useful when making a shaken cocktail with lots of fruit particles or when serving a drink up in a cocktail glass to eliminate ice shards, pulp, and herb pieces.

Hold the metal sieve over the cocktail glass and pour the cocktail from the shaker fitted with the Hawthorne strainer through the sieve and into the glass.

LAYERING TECHNIQUE

Some cocktail recipes (such as whiskey cocktails with a cream float or New York sours) call for layering the ingredients in the cocktail glass. A layer is created by reducing the force of the liquid as it's added to the ingredients already in the glass. This is accomplished by pouring the liquid over the back of a bar spoon. With one hand, hold the spoon over the cocktail, close to the surface of the liquid, with the back of the spoon facing upward. Gently pour the cream or other layering ingredient over the back of the spoon to float the layer on top.

SPANKING

To wake up and brighten herb garnishes, slap a sprig of herbs against your palm or wrist. It sounds naughty, but spanking uses the friction of the herb against the skin to lightly bruise the herb and release its aromatic compounds, making it more fragrant as you sip the cocktail.

EXPRESSING A CITRUS PEEL

Expressing a citrus peel is critical to whiskey cocktails like the old-fashioned and the Manhattan, and it is easy to do. Peel a slice of citrus skin that's mostly peel with just a little bit of pith. Hold it horizontally over the drink with the first finger and thumb of both hands, peel side facing the cocktail. Squeeze the peel so that oils spray out over the surface of the drink. Rub the outside of the peel along the rim of the glass to cover it with oils.

Clear ice in a Classic Old-Fashioned (see page 57).

Ice: The Most Important Ingredient (Besides Bourbon)

Ice makes the cocktail by chilling the ingredients and adding water during the dilution process, melding the flavors to create a cohesive cocktail.

Bourbon enthusiasts know the importance of water. From the limestone-filtered water used in bourbon distilleries to the clear ice found at high-end craft cocktail bars, those who are serious about their whiskey are also serious about their water. Master distillers and blenders often insist on certain filtration methods for the water added to their bourbon. Water is just as serious in cocktails as it is in the whiskey business.

Ice serves two functions in the formation of cocktails. It chills the cocktail and dilutes it, making the end product 15 to 25 percent water. As all bourbon enthusiasts know, the addition of water changes the flavors and aromas of a drink, whether it's a neat pour of whiskey or a cocktail on ice.

Just as lighter, more floral and fruity tones pop out of whiskey with the addition of a bit of water, adding water to a cocktail changes its balance and flavor. Compare a sip of a rough, barrel-proof bourbon and a sip of the same bourbon after adding water. The flavors are less harsh, more melded together. If you've ever built an old-fashioned quickly in a rocks glass and sipped it without a good bit of stirring, the effect is the same. At first, the bourbon is harsh, and the sweet and bitter flavors compete against each other. But after a few more stirs and as the ice melts, those flavors combine. The whiskey's harsh edges soften, the bitters and sugar blend into the whiskey, and all the elements of the cocktail make music together.

Here's what happens in the shaker or mixing glass: As solid ice cubes hit the room-temperature liquid, melting begins. As the ice melts, dilution begins as well. Equilibrium in a cocktail occurs when it is sufficiently cold and dilution slows to a minimum. At that point, it's ready to strain and serve.

That perfect duration of dilution depends on the size and type of ice used, but it occurs after 20 to 30 seconds of stirring in a mixing glass or 10 to 12 seconds of shaking. Larger ice cubes reduce the surface area of liquid hitting the ice and slow the dilution and chilling speed. When using smaller cubes, stirring or shaking time is reduced because dilution happens faster.

ICE TIPS

- Be consistent: use the same type, shape, and size of ice cubes to make and serve cocktails. This will give you greater control over the results.

- Make sure the ice is fresh to avoid the absorption of unwanted flavors from the freezer.

- When using clear ice, let it sit at room temperature for about 5 minutes before pouring the liquid over it or trying to shape it. This is called tempering. Once the outside of the cube has changed from frosty to shiny, you can use the ice however you like. If you add liquid while the ice is still very cold, the beautiful cube will crack. If you try to shape it while it's cold, it will shatter into shards.

COCKTAIL TRIVIA

Modern cocktail development depended on the availability of ice. Only in the 1800s, with the growth of the icehouse industry, were large quantities of ice shipped around the country from colder climes to warmer ones and stored in insulated buildings. Once ice became available year-round, cocktails were born. Early versions of the mint julep, thought to have originated in the South, were a combination of sugar, whiskey, shaved ice, and mint.

2 | STOCKING YOUR BAR

Shopping for Bourbon, Spirits, and Mixers

Penicillin

A classic riff on the whiskey sour, the Penicillin adds complexity with a touch of honey ginger syrup and a slightly peaty bourbon. These seasonal flavors make this a perfect sour for fall and winter cocktail parties.

2 ounces Kings County Distillery peated bourbon

1 ounce honey-ginger syrup (recipe follows)

¾ ounce fresh lemon juice

Garnish: lemon twist and Kings County single malt

Combine ingredients in a tin, shake well, and chill. Double-strain into a rocks glass seasoned with Kings County single malt over fresh ice. Garnish with a lemon twist and another spritz or float.

Honey-Ginger Syrup

1 cup fresh ginger (sliced into thin coins)

1½ cups honey

1½ cups water

Add ingredients to a pot and bring to a boil. Reduce heat to low and simmer for 1 hour. Remove from heat and cool (keep covered). Transfer mixture to quart containers (ginger included) and refrigerate. Allow to sit overnight. The following day, strain through a chinois.

New York branch of Bourbon Women—submitted by Kings County Distillery

Bourbon enthusiasts love to try new expressions and explore their bourbon palates. But it's easy to be overwhelmed as you taste your way through the hundreds of bourbons available today. Above all, keep in mind that you should use bourbons and liqueurs that *you enjoy* in cocktails. If you love a particular bourbon neat or on the rocks, it's a good choice to use in a cocktail. For most people, the whiskey they turn to on an everyday basis is a great starter for creating cocktails.

With a varied selection of bourbons and a few bottles of liqueurs, bitters, and some homemade syrups, you'll be well on your way to stocking a cocktail-friendly bar and mastering many of the classics. This chapter covers what to consider when choosing great bourbons for making cocktails, and the best part is, it involves nosing and tasting bourbons and training your palate.

One Spirit, Many Tastes

Several variables contribute to the aroma, flavor, and mouthfeel of bourbons and other whiskeys. First, there's the mash bill, or the grains used to create the distillate. For bourbon, the mash bill must be a minimum of 51 percent corn; for rye, 51 percent rye. Distillers add malted barley to contribute enzymes that convert starch into sugar. Yeast then converts the sugar into alcohol. Sometimes a third or even a fourth grain, called the flavoring grain, is added—generally either rye or wheat.

Traditional Bourbon. For most bourbons, rye is the flavoring grain. Bourbons that contain between 20 and 35 percent rye are referred to as "high-rye" bourbons. In addition to contributing spice and peppery notes to whiskey, rye changes the mouthfeel, adding a coating sensation.

Wheated bourbon. Wheated bourbons use wheat instead of rye as the flavoring grain. In general, they are softer and sweeter and have a smoother finish. Wheated bourbons can easily be overwhelmed by more aggressive flavors, but they can shine when paired with softer, delicate fruity or sweet flavors.

HOW TO TASTE BOURBON

It seems like a simple task—just take a sip! But there's more to tasting whiskey than tossing back a shot. First, slowly move the glass beneath your nose to get the aroma of the bourbon (open your mouth slightly if it's a higher-proof whiskey). Perhaps you recognize caramel, vanilla, fruit, or nut. Maybe you can smell tobacco, leather, grass, or oak. Take a few moments to savor the aromas. Now, take a sip and swallow. That first sip has a bit of a burn, and your palate has to adjust to it. Then nose the bourbon again and take another sip. Roll the bourbon around your mouth (some folks call this the Kentucky chew) and identify the flavors. Do you taste cinnamon, butterscotch, toffee, chocolate, or citrus? Does the bourbon coat the mouth, or does it feel thin? Does it burn, or is it smooth? Finally, take another sip and evaluate the finish—the feeling of the whiskey in the throat and chest, that lovely burn on the way down. Keep sipping until the glass is empty and you have a whiskey glow about you.

Rye whiskey. Different from both bourbon and high-rye bourbon, American rye whiskey must be made of at least 51 percent rye, making it spicier and more peppery than bourbon.

Wheat whiskey. American wheat whiskey must be made of at least 51 percent wheat. Wheated whiskeys tend to be soft, sweet, and nutty, and the taste of bread can often be discerned.

Aging in the Barrel

There's no substitute for time in the barrel to build flavor and aroma in whiskey. They disagree on the exact amount, but some industry experts claim that 80 percent of bourbon's flavor comes from the barrel. Atmospheric pressure and temperature push the liquid into and out of the wooden staves, altering the flavor each day as the spirit interacts with the wood. With each season, the whiskey pulls more flavor from the barrel.

Deciding when to bottle whiskey is an exercise in balance. It always involves a compromise between the positive and negative effects of aging in a barrel. Knowing exactly how long to mature a barrel of whiskey is both an art and a science that distillers spend their lives mastering. We reap the rewards of that expertise with each sip.

The most important fact about age is that, for bourborn, *age doesn't always designate quality*. Older bourbons tend to be a little drier and more complex; they often have more char or oak flavors, making them a good choice for spirit-forward and sweet cocktails. Younger, hotter bourbons play well in sours and sometimes in carbonated cocktails, as they still have enough punch to make their presence known. More important than the bourbon's age are the bourbon drinker's palate and preference.

What's Proof Got to Do with It?

I categorize whiskeys as low proof, midproof, and high proof or barrel strength. These designations are not industry categories, and they have nothing to do with how good a whiskey is or how much it costs. But for mixing cocktails at home, considering the proof of the base spirit gives you someplace to start. Proof gives whiskey its burn and heat in the mouth, as the alcohol interacts with your taste buds. It causes that fiery exhale after the first sip, especially if you're lucky enough to be tasting straight from the barrel.

At Bourbon Women events, the members tend to prefer higher-proof spirits. In 2019 Bourbon Women conducted a blind tasting where the participants (both men and women) judged the whiskeys based on nose, body,

> ## CHAR VS. TOAST
>
> Charring delivers an extremely high heat and flame to the inside of a barrel over a short period, resulting in a blackened, charred interior. Sometimes a barrel is toasted before it's charred. Toasting applies a less intense, indirect heat to the inside of the barrel over a longer period. The char of an oak barrel contributes flavors and aromas such as leather, tobacco, hay, oak, or cedar; tannic, dry, and bitter notes; and spicy flavors such as vanilla, cinnamon, and clove. Toasting reveals sweet flavors such as fruit, toffee, caramel, butterscotch, butter, bread, nuts, licorice, nutmeg, mocha, chocolate, smoke, and burnt sugar.

smoothness, complexity, and finish. Here's how the women rated the whiskeys:

Excellent: Elijah Craig Barrel Strength (124.2 proof), Wild Turkey Rare Breed (108 proof), Wild Turkey Russell's Reserve 10-Year-Old (90 proof)

Good+: Evan Williams Single Barrel 2004 Vintage (86.6 proof)

Good: Elijah Craig 12-Year-Old (94 proof), Larceny (92 proof)

Fair+: Bernheim Original Wheat Whiskey (90 proof)

Fair: Wild Turkey 81 (81 proof)

Two of the expressions that were rated "excellent" rang in at over 100 proof. This contradicts another widespread myth: that only men prefer high-proof spirits.

When tasting and nosing bourbons, proof is one of the easiest things to distinguish. A high-proof bourbon often stings the nose. For that reason, you should gently move the glass under your nose rather than sticking your nose straight into the glass. If you nose high-proof spirits too deeply, your nose may be overwhelmed, and you may need to wait half an hour or longer before evaluating any other spirits.

Proof affects cocktails in two ways. First, it determines the overall alcohol content of a drink—how strong it is. At a party, you want your guests to be able to enjoy a cocktail and still make it home responsibly. When creating cocktails for those new to bourbon, don't overwhelm their palates with high-proof spirits. A lower-proof bourbon (80–90 proof) is a good choice for bourbon newbies. Second, the higher the proof, the more aggressive the spirit is in a cocktail. Using a high-proof spirit in a delicate, fruity, or floral cocktail would overwhelm the flavors. However, that same spirit in a spicy Kentucky Bloody Mary or a smoke-forward old-fashioned would be sublime.

In this book, *low proof* refers to bourbons bottled between 80 and 90 proof. These whiskeys are generally less aggressive and less hot than higher-proof whiskeys. They do well in cocktails with more delicate flavors, where their aromas and flavors blend and build on the other cocktail ingredients. Use low-proof spirits in fruity peach and apricot and lightly floral drinks if you don't want to overwhelm the other tender elements of the cocktail.

I consider bourbons between 90 and 100 proof to be midproof whiskeys. With more

heft than low-proof whiskey in terms of flavor, they're perfect for bolder fruity, sour, and bitter cocktails in which the flavor profile of the whiskey highlights the other flavors. Midproof whiskeys are delightful in spirit-forward cocktails such as the Manhattan and the old-fashioned.

High-proof bourbons (over 100 proof and as high as the 120s for barrel-proof bourbons) can be tricky in cocktails. But if you use them wisely, you can create a tantalizing drink. High-proof whiskeys (100–105 proof) are my preference for building sours with intense fruity, bitter, or spicy profiles.

Cocktails such as the old-fashioned and the Manhattan can shine with bourbon and whiskey at any proof level, depending on the bitters and sweeteners you use. I always suggest low- or midproof bourbon when creating cocktails for bourbon newbies, but for bourbon lovers, I go with something 100 proof or higher, so the drinkers can discern the whiskey notes in the cocktail.

GO LOW PROOF WITH WARM DRINKS

Low-proof spirits are surprisingly effective in heated cocktails. In warmed cocktails such as a hot toddy or bourbon cider, more of the alcohol vapor rises from the drink, providing a burst of vanilla and baking spice flavors without increasing the overall alcohol content of the cocktail.

Choosing Which Bourbons and Whiskeys to Showcase

Choosing bourbons and whiskeys for your home bar can be a fun exercise. As you taste your way through your existing bar, think about what flavor profiles you're missing. Most important, don't save your bad whiskeys for cocktails. If you don't like a particular bourbon neat or on the rocks, you won't like it in a cocktail. If there's one

COCKTAIL LAB: WHISKEY SELECTION EXPERIMENT

Take out some of your favorite bargain or everyday bourbons and whiskeys and have someone else pour the flight for you. For this blind tasting, be sure to taste from lowest proof to highest proof. Include bourbons from the different categories listed on the opposite page, and take the time to nose and taste each one, noting the flavors and aromas. This builds a taste profile of different whiskeys you can use for constructing cocktails. Plus, you get to drink bourbon. Everybody wins!

Blind flight of bourbon prepared for evaluation.

thing you take away from this book, it should be this: use bourbon you love in your cocktails.

You'll want to have the following types of whiskeys in your bar to provide a variety of flavors and proofs when building classic and creative bourbon cocktails:

- Low-proof (80–90 proof) bourbon or whiskey

- Midproof (90–100 proof) bourbon or whiskey

- 100-proof to barrel-proof bourbon or whiskey

- Four-year-old bourbon (or with no age statement on the label, which generally means it's four years old)—young, hot whiskey

- Six- to eight-year-old bourbon—mature, complex, with a couple of layers of flavor

- Eight+-year-old bourbon, if you can find it at a reasonable price

- Wheated bourbon

- High-rye bourbon

- Rye whiskey

Did I just tell you to go out and buy nine bottles of whiskey? No. Often one bourbon fits several categories. For example, Old Forester Signature is 100 proof and high rye; Maker's 46 is wheated, midproof, and averages four to six years in the barrel.

Another way to make your selection is by flavor profile. Because flavor and aroma palates are so personal, I'll refrain from making suggestions and let you explore bourbons and ryes that fit the following flavor profiles:

- Floral
- Fruity
- Nutty
- Oak, char

- Leather, funk
- Vanilla, caramel
- Spiced, pepper, bitter
- Citrus

Find a great whiskey bar or a bourbon buddy to create blind flights for you. Bourbon drinkers love to share their whiskeys. The goal is to choose three or four bourbons you love to sip, at a medium or low price point, and with a variety of proofs and flavor profiles. Diversity in your bourbon collection means that you can match the whiskey to the cocktail's other flavor elements.

Bitters

If you make your own old-fashioneds at home, you have a bottle of Angostura bitters or orange bitters languishing in your bar. But what are bitters, and why are they so important in cocktails?

Bitters are the equivalent of a spice rack for cocktails. They are infusions of plants—roots, barks, seeds, or leaves—in alcohol or glycerin. Flavor compounds from the plants infuse the liquid. Today's cocktail bitters contain both bittering agents and flavoring agents. The bittering agents—barks and roots such as orris root, gentian, cinchona, and wormwood—make the

HOW BITTERS BALANCE

Bitters can balance both sweet and sour flavors in food and drink, muting them when they might otherwise overwhelm. They can also tie flavor elements together. For example, if you create a fruity sour with a vanilla-forward bourbon, choosing bitters with both citrus peel and vanilla notes can tie the two flavors together. Sometimes bitters can lend an extra aroma (and therefore taste) to a cocktail. For example, a banana old-fashioned made with banana syrup and a fruity bourbon is an average cocktail. But the addition of black walnut bitters gives the cocktail the nuttiness found in a fresh loaf of banana bread. (See the Banana Bread Old-Fashioned on page 64.)

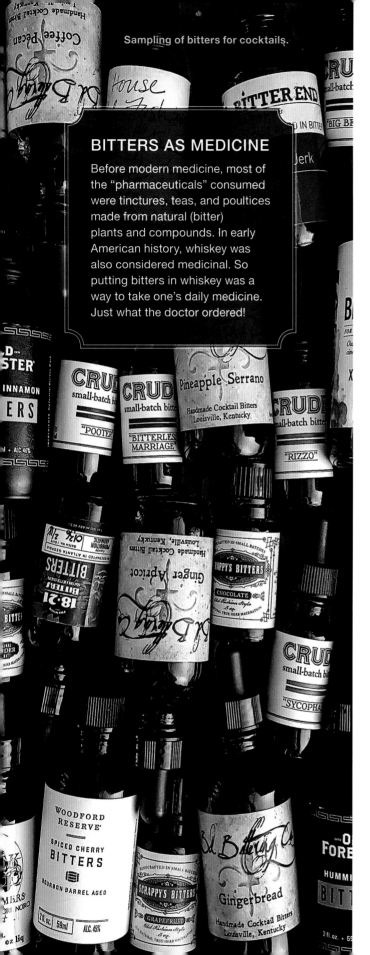

BITTERS AS MEDICINE

Before modern medicine, most of the "pharmaceuticals" consumed were tinctures, teas, and poultices made from natural (bitter) plants and compounds. In early American history, whiskey was also considered medicinal. So putting bitters in whiskey was a way to take one's daily medicine. Just what the doctor ordered!

tinctures taste bitter. Flavoring agents such as spices, herbs, fruit peels, and peppercorns add flavor. The combination results in both bitterness and aromatic notes and tastes.

Humans developed the ability to taste bitterness eons ago because so many poisonous plants and foods have a bitter taste. It was a protective mechanism to keep us alive. But over time, as humans began to discover plants and herbs with beneficial uses, we understood that bitter did not necessarily mean bad and could actually be healing.

Bitterness is a flavor that intrigues us in small quantities. Whether it's the lizard brain in all of us saying, "It's dangerous; give me more," or just a human compulsion for bitter tastes is unknown. But when you take a sip of a cocktail that has a hint of bitterness, the human response is not revulsion. Rather, it's an attraction that often opens the senses to other flavors.

ABOUT BITTERS AND BOURBON

In bourbon cocktails, bitters are used to counteract both sweet and sour elements. Their purpose is never to overwhelm but to highlight the whiskey, exposing its flavor notes and aromas. When used correctly, bitters make the bourbon shine.

One of the primary uses of bitters in bourbon cocktails is to cut down on the sweetness of the spirit. Bitters therefore go hand in hand with many great whiskey drinks. Bitters also perform two other functions in a whiskey cocktail. First, they bind the drink together as a cohesive whole. Their aromatic complexity ties the disparate elements of a drink together. For example, the licorice notes in bitters combine with the licorice rinse in a Sazerac, while the spiced pepper flavors in the bitters meld with the rye whiskey base. Tying these elements together makes the Sazerac cocktail balanced and centered.

Second, bitters can add flavors that might be missing. For example, the focused aromas and tastes of chocolate bitters, peach bitters, or celery bitters can stand in for other ingredients. To

COCKTAIL LAB: BITTERS TASTING EXPERIMENT

Not all bitters taste the same. To perform a bitters taste test, get out your bottles of bitters and a glass of unflavored, iced soda water for each one. Put two dashes of bitters in each glass and stir. Take the time to nose and taste each sample. Note the difference between what you taste and what you smell.

Next, taste each of the bitters undiluted. Place a drop on the back of your hand and taste it. Some will taste sweet, others bitter; some might be thin, others thick or creamy. Each one will perform differently in a cocktail. Tasting them diluted and cold in a small glass gives you an idea of how the bitters will behave in a cocktail, but tasting them undiluted gives you a better idea of the intensity and flavor volume and how they will react with other elements in the cocktail.

To see how two different bitters play together, add them to a fresh glass of ice and unflavored soda. I love the combination of chocolate bitters and black walnut bitters, or orange bitters and ginger bitters. What interesting taste and smell associations can you create?

To taste-test bitters, add a dash or two to iced soda water.

BITTERS IN THE CLASSIC OLD-FASHIONED AND MANHATTAN

Two of the most iconic whiskey cocktails, the old-fashioned and the Manhattan, rely on bitters to balance the sweetness of the ingredients and infuse the cocktail with aromatic complexity. For the old-fashioned, the bitters counteract the combined sweetness of the whiskey and simple syrup or sugar. They pull forward notes of citrus, licorice, and baking spice. In the Manhattan, both the whiskey and the vermouth are sweet, and the cocktail is uninteresting without bitters. They add a bold aromatic flair, push aside the sweetness of the cocktail, and enhance the tiny bit of sourness from the sweet vermouth. To test this, try making an old-fashioned or a Manhattan without bitters. The cocktail will taste flat and uninteresting.

make a chocolate-orange old-fashioned, rather than using an orange liqueur and a chocolate liqueur, I could choose a whiskey with those notes and add orange and chocolate bitters. The bitters trick the taste buds into perceiving both flavors more intensely, without adding sweet liqueurs.

BASIC BITTERS

Given the recent renaissance of bitters in all their variations, it's helpful to divide them into four basic categories: aromatic, citrus, flavoring, and savory.

Aromatic. Aromatic bitters include the classics: Angostura, Boker's, and Peychaud's. Their main characteristic is their broad aromatic compounds; they give off notes of cinnamon, clove, licorice, allspice, and ginger. Aromatic bitters add depth and complexity to cocktails.

Citrus. Orange bitters are brilliant in whiskey cocktails. They highlight the citrus and dried fruit notes in the base spirit, bringing out those flavor profiles behind bourbon's more dominant vanilla, oak, and caramel flavors.

Flavoring. Flavoring bitters focus on adding a single flavor component or a collection of flavor components to a cocktail. Chocolate bitters, coffee bitters, ginger bitters, and peach bitters all fall into this category.

Savory. Though not as common as aromatic and citrus bitters, savory bitters are a subset of flavoring bitters that focus on savory elements such as smoke, heat, vegetable, or salt.

To start stocking your bar, you'll need just a few basic bitters that blend well in bourbon and whiskey cocktails.

Angostura bitters. If a cocktail recipe calls for bitters and doesn't specify a type, it's referring to Angostura bitters. For a long time, this was the only type of bitters available—especially during Prohibition.

Peychaud's bitters. Developed in 1838 by Antoine Peychaud, a Haitian living in New Orleans, Peychaud's bitters are a classic ingredient in the Sazerac cocktail. Legend has it that Peychaud sold his bitters in a bit of cognac in a coffeehouse in New Orleans, developing the basic formula of the cocktail that is still enjoyed today.

ANGOSTURA TRIVIA

The company was able to remain in business during Prohibition by convincing the US government that bitters were nonpotable—that is, no one would drink bitters straight. This was an important clarification because bitters are often 40 percent alcohol. Angostura won the argument and remained in business throughout Prohibition.

Orange bitters. Citrus bitters meld well with whiskey, and in a whiskey sour or an old-fashioned, they balance the sweetness of the cocktail without adding too many earthy or spicy aromas.

Flavoring bitters. To get you started, I recommend at least one flavoring bitters. Choose a flavor that you love, such as chocolate, black walnut, or ginger.

INTERMEDIATE BITTERS

Once you've mastered the flavors and aromas of the most common bitters, it's time to branch out into other flavors that pair well with bourbons and whiskeys.

Chocolate bitters. These bitters bring earthy, bitter, deep chocolate flavors to a cocktail and can simulate the flavor of cocoa without adding sweetness.

Fruit bitters. Some bourbons and whiskeys burst with fruit flavors. Adding cherry, peach, or apple bitters highlights the inherent fruit notes in the whiskey and makes these delicate flavors more perceptible in a cocktail.

Nut bitters. Some great choices are pecan bitters, walnut bitters, or aromatic bitters with a strong nut flavor.

Smoke bitters. Smoke bitters enhance the char and smoke notes apparent in some whiskeys, adding a savory note to cocktails. One of my favorite bitters to add to whiskey cocktails is Hella Bitters smoked chili bitters. They add a slight tinge of smoke and a bit of heat and can stand up to a higher-proof bourbon.

ADVANCED BITTERS

Are you looking for more adventurous flavor pairings and cocktail experiments? Adding the following bitters to your inventory can open up the possibilities.

Spice bitters. Some bitters focus on a single spice aroma and flavor, such as cinnamon or ginger. Less common spices such as cardamom, chili, and Chinese five-spice can be trickier to pair with whiskey cocktails.

Floral bitters. Small amounts of lavender, chamomile, jasmine, rose, and other floral bitters delight the senses in whiskey cocktails. They're best used in conjunction with citrus cocktails such as sours to balance out the sweetness.

Woody bitters. Bourbon lovers often detect woody notes in bourbon and other whiskeys. Cedar, oak, and char-focused bitters can add to this flavor.

TIPS FOR USING BITTERS IN COCKTAILS

Start slowly. You can always add more bitters, but once you've used too many drops or dashes, you can't go back.

Make sure the bottle top is secure. If your bitters bottle has a cap with a small hole in the center, ascertain that it's secure. Otherwise, you might end up pouring bitters straight into your cocktail.

Dash vigorously. A dash is not a gentle motion. Use a decisive, quick, downward flick of the bottle to shake out the bitters.

Do the sniff test. If you aren't sure which bitters to use, mix the cocktail (minus the bitters and ice) in a mixing glass. Nose the cocktail, then nose the bitters. If the two scents play well together, the flavors will likely pair well too. Make a test cocktail.

Dashes vs. drops. Pay attention to whether your recipe calls for dashes or drops of bitters, and note whether your bottle has a dasher top or a dropper. To convert dashes to drops, I generally use 8–10 drops as the equivalent of a dash.

Espresso Manhattan (see page 87).

Salt. Though not technically bitters, adding salt in the form of a saline solution can balance both sour and bitter flavors that are overwhelming a cocktail. Sometimes just a few drops of a saline solution can achieve balance.

There are thousands of different types of bitters available on the market today. Take advantage of this bitters explosion to try new combinations of flavors and come up with inventive ways to use bitters in cocktails. Bitters can easily expand the flavor profiles of your cocktails. And they're used in such small quantities that a bottle can last for years.

Liqueurs and Spirits

The longer your fascination with cocktails lasts, the larger your collection of whiskeys, liqueurs, and spirits grows. However, with just a few bottles of liqueurs and fortified wines, you'll be ready to mix plenty of whiskey classics. Start with some basics that pair well with whiskey.

Cherry liqueur. From Cherry Heering to Luxardo Maraschino Liqueur, cherry liqueurs are often added to bourbon cocktails because of the magical pairing of bourbon and cherry. Other berry liqueurs, such as Chambord, are also excellent matches.

Orange liqueur. Whether it's Cointreau, Combier, Grand Marnier, Triple Sec, or Curaçao, an orange liqueur is critical for many whiskey cocktails. Adding a splash of orange liqueur in a sour can dramatically change the flavor profile for the better.

Coffee or chocolate liqueur. Whether you lean toward coffee or chocolate, both pair well with bourbon and rye whiskey. Buy liqueurs that are not cream based; this gives you the option of adding these flavors to cocktails without curdling the cream.

Nut liqueur. Amaretto, hazelnut, and pecan liqueurs all deserve a place in bourbon cocktails. Choose one based on your palate and preferences.

Bitter liqueurs. Campari, amari, and red bitters fall into this category. If you love Negronis, hang on to that Campari; you'll be using it for a Boulevardier.

Vermouth. Vermouths can be sweet or dry. For a classic Manhattan, you'll need sweet vermouth. For a Perfect Manhattan, you'll need both sweet and dry. Whichever you prefer, keep your opened vermouth bottles in the fridge, and consume them within about a month.

Juices

Fresh fruit juices can make the cocktail. For a sour, a smash, or a mule, fresh citrus juice makes all the difference. If you can, *always* juice limes or lemons just before building the drink. Fresh juices turn bitter after 10 to 12 hours, so taste-test any citrus juice if it has been standing around for a while. Make sure it's still brightly sour with a nice pucker.

Garnishes: Adding Flair to the Drink

Garnishes should not be an afterthought. They are critical to build visual interest and tie the drink's aromatic elements together. Most whiskey cocktails can be beautifully garnished with a citrus peel, cocktail cherries, or an assortment of nuts and dried spices. You can create striking garnishes with fancy elements, but you likely have the basics at home. Here's what I have on hand in the pantry and fridge to use as garnish:

- Cherries—nice cocktail cherries, not the cheap neon red ones

- Citrus—orange, lemon, and occasionally lime

- Dried spices—cinnamon sticks, nutmeg, and star anise

- Dried fruit—apples, pineapples, apricots, dates, and figs

Toasted S'mores Old-Fashioned (see page 66).

- Fresh fruit—pears, apples, and berries

- Sprigs of herbs

To be more extravagant, use the following to make some fantastic garnishes:

- Crushed candies

- Toasted nuts

- Candied fruits

- Small cookies or chocolate candies

- Chili or citrus powder rims

- Colored salt or sugar

- Smoked salts, sugars, and herbs

TIPS FOR MAKING SIMPLE SYRUPS

Add sugar by weight, not volume. If you're using a cup of water, measure 8 ounces of sugar for the simple syrup.

Always store syrups in a clean glass jar in the fridge.

Syrups will last 3–4 weeks in the fridge, but if they turn cloudy or become moldy, or if they smell or taste off, throw them out.

To keep syrups fresh longer, add ½–1 ounce of vodka. This extends their shelf life in the fridge from a few weeks to a couple of months.

Syrups: The Secret Flavor Weapon

Simple syrups are the unsung heroes of the home bar. They are cheap and fast to make; many don't even require cooking. They can transform a classic cocktail by adding an infusion of flavor. Think of an old-fashioned with maple syrup, a classic sour with blackberry syrup, or your favorite highball with a touch of peach-basil syrup.

BASIC SIMPLE SYRUPS

Simple syrup. Add one part sugar to one part warm water in a small jar. Shake until the sugar has dissolved.

Demerara syrup. Add one part demerara sugar to one part warm water in a small jar. Shake until the sugar has dissolved.

Brown sugar syrup. Add one part light brown sugar to one part warm water in a small jar. Shake until the sugar has dissolved.

Rich simple syrup. Add two parts sugar to one part warm water in a small jar. Shake until the sugar has dissolved.

Honey syrup. Add two parts honey to one part warm water in a small jar. Shake until the honey has combined with the water.

Sorghum syrup. Add three parts sorghum to one part warm water in a small jar. Shake until the sorghum has combined with the water.

SPICE-INFUSED SYRUPS

Spice infusions are an easy way to vary your cocktails. I love to play with the flavors in old-fashioneds, whiskey sours, and mint juleps by experimenting with spice- and herb-infused simple syrups. Here are some fun combinations:

Peach-Rosemary Sour
(see page 133).

- Vanilla and cinnamon

- Maple and cardamom

- Chai tea spiced with cinnamon, peppercorn, allspice, star anise, vanilla, or clove

- Mint and lemon thyme

- Lemon verbena or lemongrass and basil

Dry spices such as cinnamon, cardamom, vanilla, peppercorn, and the like work best if simmered on the stove with the syrup over heat. Heat 1 cup of water with 8 ounces of sugar and add 2 to 3 tablespoons of spice to the saucepan. Simmer for 10 minutes, then turn off the heat and cool completely. Taste-test as the syrup cools to ensure that your preferred flavor profile has been achieved. Strain and store in a clean glass jar.

Fresh herbs such as basil, mint, rosemary, and thyme are more delicate and don't need to be simmered. They can just steep in the saucepan as the syrup cools. Heat 1 cup of water with 8 ounces of sugar and stir to combine. Let the mixture come to a simmer; add 3 to 5 large

FRUIT SIMPLE SYRUPS

FRUIT	PROCESSING TYPE	COMMENTS
Banana	Hot	
Blackberry	Hot	
Blueberry	Cold or hot	Cold process for a tarter syrup; hot process for a sweeter syrup
Cherry	Cold or hot	Cold process for the taste of fresh cherries; hot process for the taste of cooked cherries
Peach	Cold or hot	Cold process for a tarter, fresh peach taste; hot process for a sweeter peach-cobbler flavor
Pear	Hot	
Pineapple	Cold or hot	Cold process for a bright yellow, vibrantly sweet syrup; hot process for a more caramel-tasting syrup
Strawberry	Cold or hot	Cold process for the bright, sweet taste of fresh strawberries; hot process for the flavor of jam
Watermelon	Cold	

Blackberry-Sage Smash
(see page 186).

sprigs of clean, fresh herbs; stir; and turn off the heat. Let the mixture steep as it cools to room temperature. Strain and store in a clean glass jar.

TEA SYRUPS

Some of the easiest simple syrups require nothing more than a cup of strongly brewed tea. To make a tea-based simple syrup, I double or triple the number of tea bags I normally use in a cup of water and let the tea steep until the flavors are strong but not overly bitter. Then I add a cup of sugar for each cup of brewed tea.

This makes a fantastic mint tea syrup, chai tea syrup, cinnamon tea syrup, chamomile tea syrup, and many more. The sky's the limit. You can also use leftover coffee to make a coffee simple syrup in the same way.

FRUIT SYRUPS

There are two easy ways to make syrups from fruit. One requires a stove; the other requires just a ziplock bag or plastic container. The two methods produce vastly different flavors. Consider the taste of strawberries in a cooked jam versus the taste of fresh sugared strawberries over angel food cake. You recognize both as strawberry, but the flavors are wildly different.

To use the hot process, heat the fruit in a saucepan with sugar and a little water and cook for 10 to 15 minutes on low heat until the fruit starts to break down and the juice is vibrantly colored. I usually use 1½ to 2 cups fruit, ½ cup water, and 1 cup sugar, but it varies based on the water content and sweetness of the fruit. Let the fruit cool; then strain out the pulp, pressing to remove as much of the sweet juice as possible. Store in a clean glass jar.

To use the cold process, place the chopped fruit in a ziplock bag. Add sugar: I usually use 1 cup of sugar to 1 pint of fresh sliced fruit. Seal the bag and let it sit in the fridge for about 24 hours. Strain the juice into a clean jar, pressing to remove as much of the sweet juice as possible.

See the accompanying table for a list of fruit simple syrups that play well in bourbon and whiskey cocktails.

COMBINATION SYRUPS

Even more interesting are syrups made from a combination of fruit and spices or herbs. For a peach-basil simple syrup, use the hot process to cook the peaches; when you turn off the heat, add the basil and let the mixture steep until it has cooled to room temperature. To make a pear-cinnamon simple syrup, add the cinnamon sticks and pears to the water at the same time. Let the syrup cool to room temperature before straining.

◦——◇✕◇——◦

You now have the basics: bourbons, bitters, liqueurs, and syrups. The next step is to go beyond this basic list and start developing and enjoying your own bourbon cocktails at home.

Enjoying a cocktail at a Bourbon Women event. (Photo by Four Roses Bourbon)

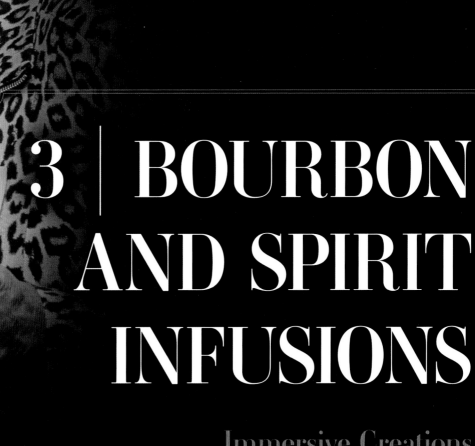

3 | BOURBON AND SPIRIT INFUSIONS

Immersive Creations

Old-Fashioned Mountain Girl

This cocktail is like Colorado women: outdoorsy and sweet with a little kick. The pine notes from the simple syrup are subtle, and the addition of chocolate bitters creates a great contrast with the herbal notes of the syrup. This simple build-in-a-glass cocktail is a great flavor combination that celebrates Colorado and its whiskey traditions.

2 ounces Old Elk blended bourbon whiskey

½–¾ ounce pine simple syrup (recipe follows; start with ½ ounce and add more to taste)

3 dashes Aztec chocolate bitters

Garnish: Luxardo cherry and small sprig of pine

Pour bourbon, simple syrup, and bitters into a whiskey glass. Stir to combine. Add ice cubes to the glass. Garnish.

Pine Simple Syrup

1 cup sugar

1 cup water

1 cup pine needles

Collect pine needles—the fresher the better—and remove them from the branch. You can use needles from spruce, balsam, Douglas fir, or white pine. The pine flavor will be softer if you collect the needles during the winter months.

Bring ingredients to a boil. Stir until sugar and water are fully combined. Remove from heat. Steep needles in syrup for at least 2 hours (overnight is better). Strain using cheesecloth, and discard the needles. Transfer the syrup to an airtight container. The syrup will keep in the refrigerator for 1 month. (Pine simple syrup can also be purchased online.)

Colorado branch of Bourbon Women—submitted by Nancy Roberts

Old-Fashioned Mountain Girl
(see page 38).

Bourbon lovers want more than just a recipe: they want layered flavors, they want to experiment, and they want to experience. Nothing is quite so experimental as making spirits infused with spices, herbs, or fruit. These infusions can be as varied as the ingredients: spices such as cinnamon, ginger, or clove; fresh, frozen, or dried fruit; and even cookies or candies.

Before starting a bourbon infusion, taste-test the bourbon for flavor and aroma notes and consider which flavors would pair well with the base spirit. For example, if you're using a smoky, oak-forward whiskey, avoid delicate herbal or floral flavors that would be obscured by the dryness of the oak notes. Fruits that burst with flavor when grilled, such as peaches, apples, and pineapples, make a vibrant infusion with a smoky or oaky bourbon. The caramelized sugars from the grilled fruit amplify the smoky notes. For spirits with more delicate floral or herbal notes, consider infusions with complementary aromas and flavors rather than heavy or aggressive elements.

Great infusions can be the result of weeks of planning and execution, or they can be happy accidents in the kitchen with a leftover bottle of bourbon. Some of my best infusions were created when I took a bite of something and thought, I wonder what would happen if I infused this in whiskey? If you love playing with flavors, bourbon infusions can be your playground.

Joy Perrine of Jack's Lounge in Louisville is considered the grandmother of bourbon infusions. To read about some of her earliest bourbon infusions, pick up a copy of the book she cowrote with Susan Reigler called *The Kentucky Bourbon Cocktail Book.*

PROFESSIONAL TIP

How long to infuse? When making infusions, longer is not always better. With teas, shorter infusion times are preferred. For instance, if black tea is infused too long, the results can be overly bitter and very tannic. The same is true of some spices such as clove, cinnamon, and allspice—if you leave them too long in an infusion, they can overpower the other flavors and tilt the flavor profile into bitterness. Your palate is your best friend when deciding how long is long enough. Trust your senses—you know what you like.

What Happens in an Infusion?

At its most basic, an infused spirit is created by the addition of flavoring agents. The alcohol (which is a solvent) strips out the flavors and aromas of the flavoring agents, and those molecular particles blend with the whiskey. Alcohol's ability to pull out the scent and flavor of cinnamon from a cinnamon stick, the sharp bite of clove, or the dryness of black tea allows you to use bourbon to concoct your own flavored spirits.

The best flavoring agents for whiskey infusions tend to be the same aromas and flavors detected when you nose and taste the whiskey itself. Orange peel, cinnamon, vanilla, and toasted nut flavors are present in many bourbons and whiskeys. Adding these flavoring agents to whiskey builds on these notes or introduces flavors that you already know play well together. Here are some of my favorite items to use in whiskey and bourbon infusions:

- Fruits: peach, apple, banana, pear, plum, pineapple

- Berries: strawberry, cherry, blackberry, raspberry

- Baking spices: cinnamon, clove, allspice, star anise, nutmeg

- Vanilla

- Dried fruits: fig, date, apple, cherry, apricot, raisin

- Citrus peel (avoid the pith, which adds bitterness)

- Toasted nuts: pecans, walnuts, almonds, hazelnuts

- Coffee or cocoa nibs

- Ginger

- Coconut

- Cookies: oatmeal raisin, chocolate chip, shortbread, gingersnap, peanut butter

- Herbs: lavender, rosemary (both excellent for Boulevardiers), sage

- Candies: red hots, caramel, toffee, lemon drops, horehound, butterscotch

How to Make Infused Whiskey

Infusing whiskey doesn't require much time or effort, and all you need are some clean jars. But first, let's cover some of the basics.

Many factors can affect spirit infusions:

- Quality of the original ingredients

- Available surface area for the alcohol to interact with

- Length of time of the infusion

- How often the infusion is agitated

To improve the flavor and punch of a whiskey infusion, use high-quality ingredients. This includes using herbs and spices that are fresh. Fruit should be fully ripe but not overripe; if it's past its prime for mixing cocktails or cooking, it can't be salvaged for an infusion. The alcohol will only magnify the off notes, and you'll end up wasting precious spirits.

Some elements infuse much faster than others, so you have to be careful. In general, strong spices such as cinnamon sticks, cloves, and peppercorns infuse very quickly. If they are not removed in time, they can overpower the

PROFESSIONAL TIP

To speed up and intensify the infusion process, cut fruit into slices or small pieces and crack spices before adding them to the whiskey. This increases the surface area with which the whiskey is able to interact. For example, a thinly sliced apple infuses faster and more effectively than a quartered apple dropped into a jar. When working with berries, muddle them a bit to crack some of them open and increase the available surface area.

For herbs, use dried rather than fresh leaves for most spirit infusions. If you use fresh basil, for example, the whiskey may turn brown and smell muddy or off. Mint is a little more forgiving, but sticking with dried herbs yields the most consistent results. If you must use fresh herbs, infuse them for just a few hours and double-strain.

PROFESSIONAL TIP

Start small. When you first start making infusions, work in small batches until you feel comfortable with the process. Begin with ½- or 1-cup jars, and work up to a 2-cup mason jar if you're feeling up to the challenge. If you're unsure how an infusion will taste, I recommend experimenting with a 1-cup infusion.

Jars prepped for the addition of whiskey for infusions.

entire infusion. When using more potent spices, it's imperative to check the flavor each day.

Here's the basic process for creating an infusion:

1. Add the infusing elements to the jar (note the amount).

2. Add the bourbon or whiskey (note the amount).

3. Seal the jar securely and label it with the date, the infusing elements, and the whiskey used.

4. Agitate the jar.

5. Put the jar in a cool, dark place.

6. Taste-test the infusion after a day or two. To speed up the process, agitate each day.

7. When the flavor reaches the desired level, strain out the infusing elements using a metal sieve, a nut-milk bag, or cheesecloth. For infusing elements with a high fat content, strain a second time.

8. For the second strain, line a metal sieve with a damp coffee filter and pour the infusion through the filter-lined sieve. For a high-fat item like a shortbread cookie, this can take hours, so you may want to leave it overnight.

9. Bottle the infusion in a clean jar; label and date it.

10. Update your notes with the straining method used, how the infusion tastes, and suggestions for next time.

> **How much will an infusion yield?** The yield varies, based on the infusing elements. When infusing with spices, you get almost all the whiskey back after straining; with fruit, expect to get less. When straining soft fruits and berries, press them lightly to get all the bourbon hiding in the fruit. When infusing with decadent, high-fat desserts or cookies, you'll lose even more of the spirit. However, the creaminess and mouthfeel of the bourbon are worth it.

The infusion time varies, based on the factors listed earlier. Spice infusions can take anywhere from two to seven days. Fruit infusions take longer—from five days to a couple of weeks. If I'm infusing peach and cinnamon sticks together in bourbon, I remove the cinnamon sticks after two or three days and leave the peaches for another week or two

Whiskey infusions can be consumed on their own, but they shine in cocktails. I try out new infusions in whiskey sours, old-fashioneds, Manhattans, Sazeracs, juleps, and highballs. If a cocktail recipe calls for a liqueur with a similar flavor profile, I substitute one of my own infused spirits for the liqueur.

COCKTAIL LAB: INFUSION STARTER EXPERIMENT

Take three ½- or 1-cup jars. In the first jar, put 1 cracked cinnamon stick. In the second jar, put 2 tablespoons of toasted, unsalted chopped nuts such as almonds or pecans. In the third jar, put 3–5 slices of very ripe banana or 2 tablespoons of tart chopped apple. Add 4–8 ounces of bourbon, depending on the size of the jar. After 24 hours, taste-test each one. If it's ready, strain it. If it needs more time, agitate it and let it sit for another day. Continue until you love the taste of the infusion.

High Tea Toddy (see page 193).

Spice Infusions

Orange- and Vanilla-Infused Bourbon

Vanilla-infused bourbon is popular (and many Bourbon Women use it as a substitute for vanilla extract), but adding a citrus peel makes the bourbon shine in old-fashioneds and sours, and it doesn't drown out other floral and oak notes. This infusion of both orange and vanilla is great in Manhattans and in winter-themed old-fashioneds.

1 vanilla bean

Peel of 1 orange (no pith)

2 cups bourbon

Split the vanilla bean with a knife and scrape out the seeds. Place the seeds, bean, orange peel, and bourbon in a clean glass jar. Seal and agitate slightly.

Store in a cool, dark place. Agitate and check every 24 hours. Usually ready in 3–7 days.

Strain with a metal sieve into a clean glass jar. Store in a cool, dark place.

Chai Spice–Infused Bourbon

Tea infusions can quickly turn a spirit dry and tannic, so this one uses a combination of spices to impart the chai flavor. I based this recipe on an herbal chai tea I make. If the peppercorns or cloves start to overpower the infusion, pull them out before the rest of the ingredients. This infusion continues to strengthen for a few days after the ingredients have been filtered out.

2 cups bourbon

1 cracked nutmeg seed

1 teaspoon vanilla extract or 1 vanilla bean

3 cracked cinnamon sticks

3 cloves

5 allspice berries, bruised

6 cardamom pods, bruised

8 peppercorns, bruised

Cracked refers to breaking spices up into small pieces with either a hammer or a rolling pin. *Bruised* refers to hitting spices or pods with a mallet, not hard enough to break them into pieces but just enough to get them to release their aromatics.

Place ingredients in a clean glass jar. Seal and agitate slightly.

Store in a cool, dark place. Agitate and check every 24 hours. Usually ready in 24–72 hours.

Strain with a metal sieve into a clean glass jar. Store in a cool, dark place.

Peppercorn-Infused Crème de Cacao

Although this recipe doesn't use whiskey, infusing your favorite chocolate liqueur or crème de cacao with peppercorns adds heat, bite, and some fun cracked-pepper notes. Added to whiskey cocktails, this infusion amps up the flavor and heat to make a stellar chocolate Manhattan or old-fashioned. Note that if you use a light crème de cacao, the peppercorns will turn it dark brown as it infuses.

1 cup dark crème de cacao

1 tablespoon peppercorns, bruised

Place ingredients in a clean glass jar. Seal and agitate slightly.

Store in a cool, dark place. Agitate and check every 12 hours. Usually ready in 24–48 hours.

Strain with a metal sieve into a clean glass jar. Store in a cool, dark place.

Tea Infusions

Using your favorite teas to infuse spirits couldn't be easier, but you have to watch them closely. Black tea infusions take just 5 to 15 minutes; any longer and you risk overpowering the infusion with dry tannic notes or woody bitterness. Some herbal teas that don't contain any white, black, or green tea can be infused longer.

For tea infusions, quickly dip the tea bag in hot water to activate it; then drop it into the spirit. Taste every 5 minutes until the flavor is perfect.

Chai Tea–Infused Bourbon

To shorten the infusion time, use a bag of chai tea with black tea in it. In addition to the chai spice notes, you'll get a good bit of tea flavor. Be sure to pull the tea bag out as soon as the taste leans toward tannic.

1 chai tea bag

1 cup bourbon

Dip the tea bag in very hot water, then immediately put it in the bourbon to steep.

Taste at 5, 10, and 15 minutes to test the flavor. If it's an herbal chai tea, the infusion can take up to an hour or so.

When you're satisfied with the flavor, remove the tea bag, put the infused bourbon in a clean glass jar, and store it in a cool, dark place.

Earl Grey–Infused Bourbon

One of my favorite tea infusions is bourbon infused with Earl Grey. To get a strong Earl Grey flavor, use bourbon in the 80- to 90-proof range and infuse it until you taste a bit of tannin in each sip. This makes the bourbon dry, but it also gives cocktails an Earl Grey finish. Use it as a base for an old-fashioned, a hot toddy, or, if you're feeling adventurous, a Boston sour.

1 Earl Grey tea bag	**1 cup bourbon**

Dip the tea bag in very hot water, then immediately put it in the bourbon to steep.

Taste at 5, 10, and 15 minutes to check the flavor.

When you're satisfied with the flavor, remove the tea bag, put the infused bourbon in a clean glass jar, and store it in a cool, dark place.

Chamomile-Infused Bourbon

Most people either love or hate chamomile, and its distinctive flavor means that it should be used judiciously in cocktails. This infusion shines in a Black Manhattan with an herbal amaro such as Cynar.

1 chamomile tea bag	**1 cup bourbon**

Dip the tea bag in very hot water, then immediately put it in the bourbon to steep.

If the chamomile tea contains black tea, taste at 5, 10, and 15 minutes. With black tea, dry tannic notes become prevalent at around 15 minutes.

If the chamomile tea is 100 percent herbal, taste at 10, 15, 30, and 60 minutes. Continue infusing until you attain the perfect flavor.

When you're satisfied with the flavor, remove the tea bag, put the infused bourbon in a clean glass jar, and store it in a cool, dark place.

How to taste-test infusions: Instead of sipping from the infusion vessel, use a straw or a bar spoon to take a small taste. This keeps the infusion germ free.

Orange Breakfast Tea–Infused Bourbon

"One lesson I've learned from all these master distillers who I really admire is to make it approachable, you know, teaching people what they can do and how to enjoy it, but not making it intimidating for them to enjoy it. Because we don't want to make it untouchable."

—Peggy Noe Stevens, founder, Bourbon Women

For some tea lovers, orange pekoe starts the day. Because it contains black tea, this infusion can quickly turn too tannic, so watch it carefully.

1 orange pekoe breakfast tea bag	1 cup bourbon

Dip the tea bag in very hot water, then immediately put it in the bourbon to steep.

Taste at 5, 10, and 15 minutes to test the flavor.

When you're satisfied with the flavor, remove the tea bag, put the infused bourbon in a clean glass jar, and store it in a cool, dark place.

Fruit Infusions

My favorite bourbon infusions are fruit infusions. I love to ramp up the apple, stone fruit, or dried fruit flavors of my favorite sips. For fruit infusions, you can use fresh fruit, dried fruit, or even frozen fruit. With fresh and frozen fruit, you won't lose too much bourbon to the infusion process, but using dry fruit reduces the yield because it soaks up the bourbon.

Darker fruits such as blackberries, dates, and dried figs create magnificent infusions (Medjool date–infused bourbon makes a delectable winter cocktail), but they turn the bourbon very dark. If you're partial to amber-colored whiskey, take note of the color of the fruit you're adding and consider that it might alter the bourbon's natural hue.

Should you sweeten infusions?
I generally don't sweeten bourbon infusions because I use them as elements in other cocktails. However, I sometimes add a tablespoon or two of raw or brown sugar (to a 2-cup infusion) to brighten up the fruity or floral notes. In small quantities, sugar acts as a flavor enhancer in drinks, just as it does in food.

Peach Infusion

In the dog days of summer, I buy an extra box of peaches and put up a few quarts of peach-infused bourbon, rum, and reposado tequila. I don't always add spices, but dropping in a cinnamon stick or nutmeg for the last day or two of the infusion adds a spice layer. On the coldest nights of winter, I often start an infusion from frozen peaches, just to remind myself of the juiciness to come in a few short months.

1½ cups chopped peaches   2 cups bourbon

Place peaches in the bottom of a clean mason jar. Add bourbon. Seal and agitate. Store in a cool, dark place.

Agitate every day. Start tasting on day 3 or 4. It may take as long as 2–3 weeks, based on your flavor preference.

When the desired flavor profile is achieved, use a metal sieve to strain into a clean glass jar. Store in the fridge for up to 6 months.

Apple Pie Infusion

Celebrate apple season with a spiced apple infusion of bourbon. Depending on the type of apples and spices used, you can create an infusion that suits your palate exactly. This one keeps it simple with a couple of apples and some cinnamon, cloves, and ginger.

2 tart apples, cored and chopped   2 slices fresh ginger

3 cinnamon sticks   2–3 cups bourbon (90 proof or higher)

2 cloves   2 tablespoons brown sugar (optional)

Put cinnamon sticks, cloves, and ginger in a cheesecloth pouch. Add the pouch, apples, and bourbon to a clean mason jar.

Store in a dark place. Agitate once a day for 3–5 days. Remove the cheesecloth pouch after day 2 or 3. Taste the infusion on day 3 and continue to infuse until it has reached the optimal intensity (I infuse mine for 10–14 days).

Strain the infusion through a metal sieve lined with a coffee filter and store it in the fridge. To sweeten the spirit just a bit, add brown sugar.

Cookie Infusions

Oatmeal Cookie–Infused Bourbon

This infusion was inspired by a bottle of Old Dominick that tasted like an oatmeal cookie. It looks rather unpleasant at first—almost like a chunky beige batter—but after double-straining, you're left with a heavenly, creamy liquid. Use it in an old-fashioned with maple syrup and spice bitters (see page 70 for the recipe).

"Live life like a good bourbon—spirited, flavorful, and full of discovery."

—Gina Caruso, former ambassador for Bourbon Women, Chicago branch

4 soft oatmeal cookies	1½ cups bourbon

Break cookies into large pieces and place them in the bottom of a clean mason jar. Add bourbon, making sure it covers the top of the cookies. Seal and agitate the jar. Place it in a cool, dark place and agitate every 12 hours. Test at 24 hours, then every 8 hours thereafter. (My infusion reached perfection at 32 hours.)

Strain first through a fine metal sieve. Discard solids and clean the sieve. Next, line the metal sieve with a coffee filter and strain the infusion again. This takes about 12 hours. Put a plate or a plastic bag over the strainer and the container to limit evaporation.

Pour the double-strained bourbon into a clean glass jar and store it in the fridge for 2–3 months.

Shortbread Cookie–Infused Bourbon

Bourbon drinkers love bourbon and cookie pairings, but cookie-infused bourbon is special, adding layers of both spice and creaminess. The yield will be lower than with a spice infusion, but this makes an incredible gift for another bourbon lover.

12 shortbread cookies	3 cups bourbon

Place cookies in the bottom of a clean mason jar. Add bourbon, making sure it covers the top of the cookies. Seal and agitate the jar. Place the jar in a cool, dark place and agitate every 12 hours. Test at 24 hours, then every 8 hours thereafter. (Mine was ready at 48 hours.)

Strain first through a fine metal sieve. Discard solids and clean the sieve. Next, line the metal sieve with a coffee filter and strain the infusion again. This takes about 12 hours. Put a plate or a plastic bag over the strainer and container to limit evaporation.

Pour the double-strained bourbon into a clean glass jar and store it in the fridge for 2–3 months (but it probably won't last that long). Yields 16–20 ounces of infused bourbon.

Grandma's Oatmeal Cookie Old-Fashioned (see page 70).

4 | THE OLD-FASHIONED

The Grandmother of All Whiskey Cocktails

Bourbon Women tour the Michter's Fort Nelson Distillery in downtown Louisville during the 2019 SIPosium. (Photo by Chris Joyce KY)

Old Earl

The Old Earl is a great porch cocktail that's both easy to make and elegant to sip. The lavender bitters add bright floral notes that blend deliciously with the orange juice.

1½ ounces Buffalo Trace Kentucky straight bourbon

¾ ounce brown sugar simple syrup

1 dash Scrappy's lavender bitters

¼ navel orange, squeezed

Garnish: dehydrated orange chip

Combine bourbon, simple syrup, bitters, juice from the orange, and orange quarter in a shaker with ice. Shake to combine. Strain over a large ice cube in a rocks glass, garnish, and enjoy.

By Sable Dixon, 2018 Bourbon Women "Not Your Pink Drink" amateur winner

Now that we've covered the basics, it's time to get to the magic: making cocktails. And what better place to start than the old-fashioned? It's the grandmother of all whiskey cocktails and one of the first cocktails recorded. It's a classic drink with three simple elements—spirit, sugar, and bitters—so it's easily mastered and endlessly variable.

The sugar or simple syrup sweetens the cocktail, dropping the heat from the whiskey and adding a thicker mouthfeel. The bitters cut through the sweetness and tie the bourbon's spice notes to the bitters' earthy base notes. The aromatics of the bourbon and the bitters combine, pulling the bourbon's secondary aroma and flavor notes to the forefront. The old-fashioned is a deceptively simple cocktail made complex by the selection of a particular whiskey, sweetener, and bitters.

Although there is a classic old-fashioned recipe (see page 57), I want you to make a version that tastes good to you. If that means using a sugar cube and a muddler or substituting chocolate bitters for Angostura, do whatever it takes to create *your* perfect old-fashioned.

> ## WHISKEY TRIVIA
>
> Historically, whiskey was considered a medicine. It was used to treat pain, cough, and other symptoms of illness. Whiskey was paired with natural remedies in the form of bitter tinctures, and a dash of sugar was added to help the medicine go down. People would get up in the morning and take a dose of whiskey and bitters to cure what ailed them. Thus, the old-fashioned was often considered a morning cocktail, like mimosas or Bloody Marys today.

History of the Old-Fashioned: The Original Whiskey Cocktail

Early American whiskey was rough—eye-watering, throat-burning, cough-inducing rough. It was nothing like the smooth, barrel-aged spirit we enjoy today. Farmers took their excess grains and transformed them into a transportable, consumable product: whiskey. All they needed was some corn or rye, natural yeast, water, and a heat source.

The first written mention of the cocktail that became the old-fashioned was in Jerry Thomas's 1862 *Bar-Tender's Guide,* the first cocktail book published in the United States. He wrote of a whiskey cocktail consisting of Boker's bitters, gum syrup (an old version of sugar syrup), and a glass of whiskey, topped with a twist of lemon. Sounds familiar, doesn't it?

After the whiskey cocktail caught on, bartenders started to tinker with the recipe, adding a dash of cherry liqueur, orange curaçao, or absinthe to tweak the cocktail's flavor and balance. Later they swapped loaf or cubed sugar for the gum syrup, necessitating the use of a muddler to break it up and make a small bit of simple syrup before adding the whiskey and ice to the glass. Eventually, bartenders added pieces of fruit, such as cherries and oranges, to their muddling. The legacy of the whiskey cocktail as a fruit salad was born.

So where did the term *old-fashioned* come from? In the 1870s and 1880s, drinkers started a movement to take the whiskey cocktail back to its roots. Patrons wanted bartenders to remove the extra liqueurs, the muddled fruits, and the soda and return to the basics: whiskey, bitters, and sugar. So they would ask for an "old-fashioned whiskey cocktail." Eventually, this was shortened to simply old-fashioned and became part of the cultural lexicon.

Classic Old-Fashioned.

The Four Elements of an Old-Fashioned

Whiskey, bitters, sugar, and ice: that's all you need to make an old-fashioned. But there are considerations related to each one that can affect the composiotion of the cocktail.

Whiskey. When polled, Bourbon Women members preferred bourbon over rye as the base spirit for an old-fashioned. Each brings different characteristics to the table. Bourbon is sweeter, with more vanilla and citrus notes. However, rye's spicier notes tie into the aromatic bitters and punch up the flavor contrasts more than bourbon does.

Bitters. Angostura bitters are the classic ingredient in today's old-fashioned, but I like to use both Angostura and orange bitters (half and half). Angostura bitters add clove, star anise, and earthy tones to the old-fashioned. But to enhance the citrus notes (which I love), I add orange bitters. If you prefer nut bitters or Peychaud's bitters, use them. Consider matching the flavor profiles of the whiskey and the bitters.

Sugar. I use simple syrup in old-fashioneds because I want each sip to be equally sweet. I'd prefer not to find a lump of sugar at the bottom of the cocktail glass when sipping with a straw or tipping back for that last swallow. Simple syrup can be mixed in the bottom of a rocks glass, but I like to move fast when making a cocktail, so I depend on premade simple syrups (see chapter 2). You can use a simple syrup made with white sugar, brown sugar, or demerara sugar. You can even make gum syrup or an infused syrup.

Ice. The perfect old-fashioned is served over one large cube or ice sphere or several medium-sized cubes. A large cube keeps the cocktail from diluting too quickly if you're relaxing at home and want to linger over your old-fashioned.

Classic Old-Fashioned

2 ounces bourbon

½ ounce simple syrup or ¼ ounce rich simple syrup

3 dashes Angostura bitters

Garnish: orange peel

Add ingredients to a mixing glass. Stir 30 times. Strain into a rocks glass with one large ice cube. Express the oils from the orange peel directly over the drink and run the peel around the rim of the glass. Place the peel in the glass and serve.

Making Your Own Riff on the Old-Fashioned

Because the old-fashioned has just three main flavor elements, it's easy to create twists on the classic cocktail. Tinker with each of the variables until you find a combination you love. My passion for mixology started with the old-fashioned, and it's still a favorite of mine to experiment with. There are plenty of flavor variations to explore!

PLAY WITH THE SPIRIT BASE

Whiskey is the classic base, but feel free to choose bourbon, rye, or a combination of the two. When two spirits form the flavor base of a drink, it's referred to as a split-base cocktail. You can also choose two different bourbons or two different ryes as the base. Make sure the flavors and aromas of the two spirits play well together.

PLAY WITH THE BITTERS

My favorite way to tinker with an old-fashioned is to use different bitters. In winter I love sorghum bitters, ginger bitters, or darker nut bitters in old-fashioneds. In summer I add peach, apricot, smoke and chili, or floral bitters. To highlight the notes from the bitters, I might use an extra garnish, such as candied ginger or a toasted nut in the winter or a peach slice or fresh edible flower in the summer.

Consider combinations of bitters, such as chocolate and orange bitters or ginger and nut bitters with a spicy rye old-fashioned. Mix up the cocktail except for the bitters, then nose each bitters to determine which one is the best match (see this chapter's Cocktail Lab).

PLAY WITH THE SWEETENER

Besides varying the type of simple syrup, you can use fruit- or spice-infused syrups to make some fabulous combinations (think peach-rosemary or blackberry-basil simple syrup). To add a little more flavor variation to the old-fashioned, consider using blackberry brandy, peach liqueur, or coffee liqueur, or add some coconut for a tropical vibe. When using a liqueur in an old-fashioned, decrease the amount of whiskey to avoid making the cocktail too strong. A cocktail with four ounces of distilled spirits is twice the usual alcohol content for one drink.

So get out your whiskeys, bitters, and syrups to experiment with this classic cocktail. For each of the recipes that follow, I used these elements to create new versions of the old-fashioned. I suggest starting with your favorite foods and flavors and giving them a healthy whiskey kick. For example, one of my favorite candies is a chocolate-covered orange cream from Schimpff's Confectionery in Jeffersonville, Indiana. My early experiments with old-fashioneds used whiskey, chocolate liqueur, and orange bitters to create a cocktail version of this candy. You can do the same with savory flavors. If you love apple-smoked bacon, create an old-fashioned with apple cider syrup and smoked bitters, and garnish it with a crispy slice of bacon. Start with your favorite desserts, meals, or food pairings and think about how to incorporate those elements in a cocktail.

Breakfast Old-Fashioned (see page 67).

Setup for the old-fashioned cocktail lab.

COCKTAIL LAB: BITTERS EXPERIMENT

For this experiment, you'll need bourbon, simple syrup, four rocks glasses, ice, and three or four different kinds of bitters. I recommend Angostura, orange, chocolate, and black walnut bitters, but you can use whatever you have. If you have only three bitters, put a combination of two bitters in the fourth glass.

1. Combine 4 ounces of bourbon and 1 ounce of simple syrup in a mixing glass. Fill with ice, stir 30 seconds, then strain into the four rocks glasses with ice. You now have four half-servings of an old-fashioned. Take a sip. Not very flavorful, is it? Bitters add a critical balancing and flavoring component to the drink.

2. To the first glass, add 1 dash Angostura bitters and stir. To the second, add orange bitters, and so on until each glass contains bitters.

3. Nose and taste each old-fashioned. Note the differences between the bitters: Angostura versus orange, or chocolate versus black walnut. Take note of the different characteristics of the bourbon in each sample. There may be more nut notes with the addition of black walnut bitters or more floral notes with the orange bitters. More of the whiskey's baking spices might come through with the chocolate or Angostura bitters.

4. Now add 1 dash of a second bitters to each glass. Be creative in combining them. I love orange and chocolate together, or black walnut and chocolate. Notice how much flavor complexity the second bitters adds.

Dos and Don'ts for Making an Old-Fashioned

Do use a bourbon or whiskey you love. The whiskey is the star of the show. It's fine to use a whiskey that's not expensive, but choose one you enjoy drinking.

Do underdilute—just slightly. If you pour a perfectly diluted cocktail over ice, it may taste watery within a few minutes. I prefer to underdilute and stir for 20 seconds rather than 30, since I'll be serving the cocktail over ice. The drink should still taste like a cocktail at the last sip.

Don't add soda. An old-fashioned is served over ice, so it continues to dilute as the ice melts. There's no need to add soda. If the cocktail is too strong for you, just wait a minute or two, give the drink a quick stir, and sip.

Don't skimp on the garnish. Use fresh orange peel and high-quality cherries. Many people swear by Luxardo, Traverse City, or Bada-Bing cherries.

Do use large-format ice cubes. Even if the ice isn't clear, a large, slow-melting ice cube or ice sphere will keep the old-fashioned at its peak longer.

Do build in the glass. The classic old-fashioned is a no-fuss cocktail that can be built right in the rocks glass (although I prefer to use a mixing glass). Add bitters, syrup, and bourbon and stir. Add ice and stir until well chilled. Garnish and sip.

Perfect Old-Fashioned

This variation is my absolute favorite. I use light brown sugar simple syrup, 100-proof bourbon, and a combination of aromatic and orange bitters. I keep it traditional and express an orange peel over the top of the cocktail. This combination of simple elements highlights the whiskey and supports its citrus peel notes, while the brown sugar supports the whiskey's dried fruit flavors.

2 ounces Old Forester Signature 100-proof bourbon

½ ounce light brown sugar simple syrup

1 dash orange bitters (I use Woodford Reserve orange bitters)

1 dash Angostura bitters

Garnish: orange peel

Combine ingredients in a mixing glass and fill with ice. Stir for 20 seconds, then strain into a rocks glass with one large ice cube. Express an orange peel over the cocktail and add it to the glass.

Kentucky Smolder

Creating a great old-fashioned for serious whiskey drinkers requires finesse. You need to highlight the whiskey above everything else, balance it with great bitters, and make sure it contains a hint of intrigue to keep them interested. The smoked chili bitters add both smoke and heat from the capsaicin found in chili peppers. And through it all, the bourbon still shines. I created this high-proof old-fashioned for a Bourbon Women "He Sips, She Sips" event featuring a blind tasting of Heaven Hill bourbons and ryes.

2 ounces Old Forester Whiskey Row 1920, high-proof (110 or higher) bourbon, or Pikesville rye

½ ounce demerara sugar simple syrup

3 dashes Hella Bitters smoked chili bitters

Garnish: charred cinnamon stick

Combine ingredients in a mixing glass and fill with ice. Stir for about 20 seconds, then strain into a rocks glass with fresh ice. Garnish with a charred cinnamon stick (be careful not to set your fingers on fire).

Kentucky Smolder.

Banana Bread Old-Fashioned

This cocktail works well with any whiskey that evokes the smell of banana bread baking in the oven, as well as any bourbon with prominent vanilla and caramel notes, especially one with a little nutty undertone. This cocktail has a perfect flavor balance: it highlights the bourbon's banana notes and delves into the underlying baking spice aromas.

2 ounces Old Forester Signature 100-proof bourbon (or Old Forester 86 proof)

½ ounce banana simple syrup (recipe follows)

2 dashes Fee Brothers black walnut bitters

Garnish: orange peel and vanilla bean or cinnamon stick

Combine ingredients in a mixing glass and add ice. Stir until well chilled, about 20 seconds. Strain into a rocks glass with a large ice cube and add garnish.

Banana Simple Syrup

Try this syrup in whiskey sours, smashes, rum cocktails, or hot tea, or pour it over coffee cake or hot biscuits.

3 very ripe bananas

1 cup sugar

⅓ cup water

Add ingredients to a small saucepan and heat to a low simmer, stirring occasionally. Simmer for 10–15 minutes, or until the banana flavor starts to pop. Cool and strain into a clean glass jar. Store in the fridge.

Toasted S'mores Old-Fashioned

This recipe will be popular with both seasoned bourbon lovers and whiskey newbies. Pick a bourbon with notes of toasted marshmallow and chocolate, and add a little campfire smoke with the peated whiskey or mezcal. This is an explosion of flavors, especially with a mini s'more for garnish (see the photo on page 30). To earn bonus points, do a flavor pairing of this cocktail and actual s'mores.

1¾ ounces bourbon

¼ ounce crème de cacao or Ballotin chocolate whiskey

½ ounce toasted marshmallow simple syrup (recipe follows)

16 drops Bittermens Xocolatl mole chocolate bitters

1 bar spoon peated whiskey or smoky mezcal

Garnish: tiny s'more

Combine ingredients in a mixing glass. Add ice and stir until well chilled, about 20 seconds. Strain into a rocks glass with one large ice cube and add garnish.

Toasted Marshmallow Simple Syrup

1 cup sugar

1 cup water

12 toasted marshmallows

Combine water and sugar in a saucepan. Add marshmallows (toasted but not charred). Heat until the marshmallows are melted and the sugar is dissolved. It will still look foamy and creamy but should be fully liquid. Cool completely. Strain through a metal sieve, and spoon the foam off the top of the syrup, as it can make the cocktail cloudy. Store in the fridge for 2–3 weeks. (Torani and Monin also make a toasted marshmallow syrup that can be used for coffee, cocktails, hot chocolate, and desserts.)

Breakfast Old-Fashioned

At the Bourbon Women annual SIP-osium, mornings start with a tasting or a cocktail. And since the old-fashioned was originally a morning cocktail, why not start the day with one? This version uses the flavors of a typical American breakfast (see the photo on page 59).

2 ounces midproof bourbon

½ ounce noncreamy coffee liqueur (optional)

½ ounce coffee simple syrup (recipe follows)

1 bar spoon maple syrup (preferably barrel-aged)

2 dashes orange bitters

Garnish: maple syrup and espresso powder or finely ground coffee; orange peel; bacon (optional)

Prepare a rocks glass by putting a swipe of maple syrup on the lip and dusting it with espresso powder or finely ground coffee. Set aside. Add ingredients to a mixing glass. Fill with ice. Stir until well chilled, about 20 seconds. Strain into the prepared rocks glass filled with ice. Express an orange peel over the cocktail and add it to the glass. If you're a bacon lover, add a crispy slice of bacon as garnish.

Coffee Simple Syrup

1 cup strong or cold-brew coffee or espresso

1 cup sugar

Warm the coffee if it's cold brew. Combine coffee and sugar and stir until the sugar is fully dissolved. Cool and refrigerate in a clean glass jar. Keeps for 4 weeks.

THE NOSE KNOWS

Bourbon drinkers know the nose is king when it comes to evaluating any spirit. When selecting a whiskey or liqueur, use the nose's expertise. Before combining any other spirit, mixer, or syrup with bourbon, do a sniff test. Put a sample of the bourbon in a shot glass (or sniff directly from the bottle after agitating it), and smell the bourbon and the other potential ingredients at the same time. If they smell compatible, make a sample cocktail to taste.

Caramel Apple Old-Fashioned.

Caramel Apple Old-Fashioned

All year I wait for apple season and fresh apple cider from my local orchard. One year, I boiled 8 cups of apple cider down to 1 cup, making a concentrate known as apple cider molasses. It was magical: both tart and sweet, with the consistency of thick maple syrup. Adding it to bourbon, along with some salted caramel syrup, is like taking a bite out of a caramel apple.

2 ounces midproof bourbon

¼ ounce apple cider molasses (recipe follows)

¼ ounce salted caramel syrup

2 dashes Bittercube cherry bark vanilla bitters

1 dash Hella Bitters ginger bitters

Garnish: apple fan or wheel or caramel apple

Combine ingredients in a mixing glass and fill with ice. Stir for about 20 seconds. Strain into a rocks glass with one large ice cube. Garnish with an apple fan, a drizzle of apple cider molasses, or a whole caramel apple for a food pairing and garnish in one!

Apple Cider Molasses

Apple cider molasses is mouthwatering on everything from pancakes and biscuits to grilled meats, fresh fruit, and ice cream. Make a batch, and it will go fast. Keep in mind that some batches are very sweet; others, not so much. It depends on the apples used in the fresh-pressed cider.

8 cups fresh apple cider (do not substitute apple juice or highly filtered apple cider)

Reduce apple cider over medium heat until just 1 cup remains. Start with the cider at a fast simmer; then, as the volume reduces, turn the heat down to a light simmer. You don't want to scorch it. Cool and store in a clean glass jar in the fridge for up to 4 weeks.

Grandma's Oatmeal Cookie Old-Fashioned

 I have cookie-related trust issues stemming from grabbing cookies I thought were chocolate chip that turned out to be oatmeal raisin. But because oatmeal cookies have many of the flavors inherent in bourbon—cinnamon, baking spices, vanilla, dried fruit—I knew an oatmeal cookie–infused bourbon would shine. As soon as I tasted the infusion, I decided to use it in an old-fashioned with maple syrup.

2 ounces oatmeal cookie–infused bourbon (see recipe on page 50)

¼ ounce barrel-aged maple syrup

12 drops Old Forester smoked cinnamon bitters

Garnish: cinnamon stick; oatmeal cookie to dunk

Combine ingredients in a mixing glass with ice. Stir for 20 seconds until well chilled. Strain into a rocks glass with a large ice cube. Garnish with a cinnamon stick and serve with half a cookie (or a whole cookie or three).

Grandma's Oatmeal Cookie
Old-Fashioned.

Black Satin Old-Fashioned

 Blackberry season in Kentucky is short—just a few weeks. One day my blackberry bushes are drooping with ripe berries and then, just as suddenly, they're finished. Their peak often coincides with the first culling of the basil bushes, so this easy summer cocktail makes good use of both. Basil's licorice flavor matches well with high-rye bourbon (or rye), but the basil can be overwhelmed by a high-proof spirit. Choose a midproof spirit to allow the blackberries and basil to shine.

2 ounces midproof bourbon or rye

½ ounce blackberry-basil simple syrup (recipe follows)

2 dashes Bittercube cherry bark vanilla bitters

1–2 basil leaves

Garnish: basil leaves and fresh or frozen blackberries

Rub basil leaves on the inside and rim of a rocks glass until fragrant. Discard the leaves. Combine whiskey, simple syrup, and bitters in a mixing glass and fill with ice. Stir until very well chilled. Strain into the prepared rocks glass with ice. Garnish.

Blackberry-Basil Simple Syrup

3 cups frozen blackberries

¼ cup water

1½ cups sugar

Leaves from 3 large sprigs basil

Combine blackberries, water, and sugar in a small saucepan. Cook on medium heat until the blackberries are thawed, soft, and very juicy. As the blackberries cook down, press on them to release the juice. Reduce heat and simmer for 10 minutes. Add basil leaves, turn off the heat, and let the syrup cool completely. Strain the blackberries out, pressing on them to get as much juice as possible. Cool and store in a glass bottle in the fridge for 1–2 weeks.

Black Satin Old-Fashioned.

Lavender-Lemon Old-Fashioned.

Lavender-Lemon Old-Fashioned

Infusing the simple syrup with lemon juice and lemon peel adds tart, bright notes of lemon oil to the sweetness of the syrup. Lavender bitters add a brilliant floral note, so select a bourbon with some light floral notes.

2 ounces midproof bourbon

½ ounce lemon simple syrup (recipe follows)

12 drops Scrappy's lavender bitters

Garnish: lemon peel and lavender sprig

Combine ingredients in a mixing glass and fill with ice. Stir until the outside of the mixing glass is very cold, about 20 seconds. Strain into a rocks glass filled with ice and add garnish.

Lemon Simple Syrup

This syrup makes an incredible whiskey sour, smash, gin cocktail, highball, Tom Collins, or tea toddy.

¾ cup fresh lemon juice (peel the lemons before juicing them and reserve the peels)

¾ cup sugar

Reserved lemon peels (no pith)

Combine lemon juice and sugar in a small saucepan on medium heat. Stir until the sugar is dissolved and the syrup is at a very low simmer. Add lemon peels, stir, and let the mixture sit for 5 minutes on low heat. Turn off the heat and steep for 45 minutes. Strain out the peels. Bottle and refrigerate the syrup. It will keep 2–3 weeks in the fridge.

MISSING AN INGREDIENT?

To find an appropriate substitute for an ingredient, consider the volume, flavor, and sweetness of all the potential options. Stay in the same family of flavors and swap sweet for sweet, bitter for bitter, and sour for sour. For example, if you don't have a flavored simple syrup but you do have a liqueur of that flavor, try it—but be mindful of the overall alcohol content. Liqueur flavors can vary wildly by brand, so do a taste test first. If you're missing the specific type of bitters called for, don't omit the bitters altogether; add a similar bitters or a flavored liqueur with a general aromatic bitters. If you're missing a specialty liqueur, try a simple syrup with the same flavor. If you're missing a sour element, use a similarly acidic citrus or balsamic vinegar. Note that orange can't be substituted for lemon or lime; it won't be tart enough, and you'll need to add some citric acid.

Cran of Whoop-Ass Old-Fashioned

Around November and December, there's always some leftover cranberry sauce. Paired with muddled rosemary, a hot bourbon, and a little ginger liqueur, it makes a fun cocktail for the holidays. Adjust the amount of cranberry sauce based on how sweet it is (don't try this recipe with canned cranberry sauce). This cocktail is shaken rather than stirred to get the cranberry sauce well incorporated. It will be a little cloudy, even after straining, but don't worry about it.

1 heaping tablespoon cranberry sauce

1 sprig rosemary, torn

¼ ounce maple syrup (preferably barrel-aged)

½ ounce ginger liqueur

2 ounces 100-proof bourbon (something a little aggressive and hot)

3 dashes gingerbread bitters

Garnish: rosemary skewer with fresh cranberries

Combine cranberry sauce, rosemary, and maple syrup in a shaking tin and muddle well to break up the cranberry sauce and activate the rosemary's aromatics. Add ginger liqueur, bourbon, bitters, and ice. Shake well and double-strain into a rocks glass over one large ice cube. Garnish.

Prince Harry Old-Fashioned

Originally created for a Bourbon Women's blind tasting of Heaven Hill products, this cocktail celebrates the spice notes found in Elijah Craig small batch, but it can be made with any bourbon with lots of baking spice notes.

1½ ounces Elijah Craig small-batch bourbon

½ ounce Domaine de Canton ginger liqueur

½ ounce honey syrup

3–4 dashes Hella Bitters ginger bitters

Garnish: slice of candied ginger

Combine ingredients in a mixing glass and fill with ice. Stir and strain into a rocks glass with ice. Garnish.

Cran of Whoop-Ass Old-Fashioned.

Bourbon Women Sip 'n' Shop event, 2019. (Photo by Four Roses Bourbon)

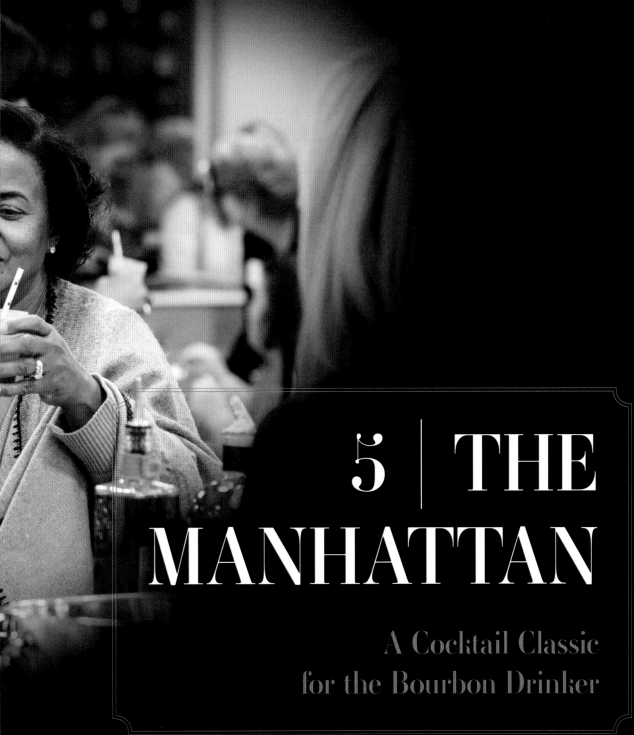

5 | THE MANHATTAN

A Cocktail Classic for the Bourbon Drinker

The Rosemary and Maggie Manhattan

Maggie Kimberl, the 2021 president of Bourbon Women, embarked on an experiment with her friend Rosemary to develop the perfect Manhattan. They tested vermouths, bitters, and different base spirits. After many experimental cocktails and a good deal of laughter, they settled on this recipe.

1½ ounces Michter's barrel-strength rye

¾ ounce Byrrh Grand Quinquina

2 dashes Angostura bitters or Woodford Reserve spiced cherry bitters

Garnish: 1 Traverse City Whiskey Co. cocktail cherry

Combine ingredients in a mixing glass with ice and stir. Strain into a coupe glass and garnish.

By Maggie Kimberl, Bourbon Women president, 2021

When not sipping their bourbon neat, members of Bourbon Women often enjoy Manhattans. A spirit-forward drink that packs a tasty whiskey punch, a well-made Manhattan can be a symphony of bourbon, vermouth, and bitters that turns the cheeks pink and releases some of the best stories from the vault. Bourbon is the star of the show. Maybe that's why early whiskey drinkers enjoyed the cocktail so much. It celebrates the elements that go into it instead of hiding bad whiskey behind other flavors.

History of the Manhattan

Like most classic cocktails, the Manhattan has an origin myth that's more interesting than the much murkier truth. Legend has it that the Manhattan was first served at a party hosted by Winston Churchill's mother in honor of a presidential candidate at the Manhattan Club in New York City. The party was so successful that people simply referred to the cocktail by the name of the club. Unfortunately, Mrs. Churchill was giving birth in Oxfordshire on the date of the party, so that story is now regarded as a myth.

What we do know is that the cocktail was born at the Manhattan Club in New York in the 1880s, although we're not sure who created it. At the time, vermouth, a fortified wine popular in Europe, had made its way to the United States and was being sold across the country. Given Americans' proclivity for mixing up cocktails, it was inevitable that whiskey and vermouth would be combined.

Many whiskey drinkers now turn to bourbon for their Manhattans, but the earliest Manhattans were likely made with rye whiskey. Its pepper, spice, and creamy mouthfeel can cut through the sweet vermouth a little better than bourbon can. Today, both bourbon and rye are used to make the classic Manhattan, and the preferred spirit is often a matter of contention among cocktail enthusiasts. But you can decide for yourself.

The Three Elements of a Manhattan

The classic Manhattan has only three ingredients: whiskey, vermouth, and bitters. It's not a complicated cocktail, but those three elements open the door to thousands of variations.

Whiskey. The Manhattan was made for whiskey, and this is not a cocktail for bottom-shelf spirits. Use a bourbon or rye you love to drink neat or on the rocks. Choose a midproof bourbon for Manhattans or one with fullness, such as Michter's, Woodford Double Oaked, New Riff, or Wilderness Trail. If you choose rye, the Manhattan will be spicy and peppery, and it will stand up to the sweetness of the vermouth.

Vermouth. Vermouth is a fortified wine infused with a proprietary blend of botanicals. Both the base wine and the botanicals drive the varied flavors of vermouths, and the recipes are highly guarded secrets. Manhattans use sweet or red vermouth (sometimes called Italian vermouth), but vermouth also comes in a dry style that is less sweet and paler in color. A third style, blanco or white, has a sweetness level between sweet and dry vermouth.

WHISKEY TRIVIA

The earliest versions of the Manhattan cocktail didn't use the now common 2:1 ratio of whiskey to vermouth. Early bartenders used equal amounts of both, with the addition of a healthy dose of bitters for balance. Today the ratio varies a bit—2–2½ ounces of whiskey to ½–1 ounce of sweet vermouth—but there's no doubt bitters should be added, along with a citrus peel or cherry for garnish.

Vermouth adds sweetness, herbal and floral notes, and slight sourness to a Manhattan. My two favorite sweet vermouths for Manhattans are Carpano Antica Formula vermouth (strong vanilla, orange, date, and chocolate flavors) and Cocchi Vermouth di Torino (cocoa, bitter orange, woody, and herbal notes). Both are very sweet, vibrant vermouths, and they pull out different aromas and flavors from different whiskeys. For a less sweet vermouth, try Dolin Rouge (citrus, dried fruit, herbaceous, and bitter notes).

Bitters. Traditionally, bartenders use Angostura bitters in a Manhattan, but there are hundreds of bitters to choose from. The bitters I use in my Manhattans depend on the specific whiskey. When mixing with Johnny Drum, I add Woodford Reserve sorghum and sassafras bitters to highlight the whiskey's cinnamon notes. If I use Woodford Reserve Double Oaked, which is full of earthy aromas, I lighten the cocktail with orange or spiced cherry bitters. To create a flavor contrast, use bitters that differ from but are complementary to the spirits in the cocktail. For example, add chocolate bitters if you get caramel notes from the whiskey, or add nut bitters when you detect banana or apple.

Creating a Manhattan isn't difficult, but it's critical to use quality whiskeys and vermouths to make each element burst with flavor. Once you've mastered the basic Manhattan, experiment by adding different liqueurs or amari to build more layers of flavor into the cocktail. Remember, a Manhattan is always stirred, never shaken.

Classic Manhattan

2 ounces bourbon

1 ounce high-quality sweet vermouth

2 dashes Angostura bitters

1 dash cherry bitters

Garnish: high-quality cocktail cherry

Add ingredients to a mixing glass. Fill with ice and stir for 30 seconds. Strain into a chilled coupe glass and garnish.

Classic Manhattan.

Making Your Own Riff on the Manhattan

The classic Manhattan is a bar staple, but the simplicity of the elements opens up the possibilities for many delicious variations. Some become standards in their own right, such as the Black Manhattan and the Perfect Manhattan. Others are simply fun riffs on the basic flavors and contrasts. Experimenting with each flavor element in the Manhattan allows you to use your imagination to build new variations.

PLAY WITH THE SPIRIT BASE

Although bourbon and rye are the standards, you can add other spirits to the mix. A great sweet-mash moonshine makes a fabulous Manhattan. Another option is to combine rye and bourbon to make the base spirit, or you can use a flavored whiskey for some of the base. Adding a little orange liqueur or bitter amaro can completely shift the balance in delectable ways. But remember that to construct a truly great Manhattan, build on the inherent flavors of the whiskey base. A great Manhattan doesn't hide the whiskey—it highlights it.

PLAY WITH THE BITTERS

Bitters add flavor, balance, contrast, and complexity. When building a Manhattan, consider a combination of bitters to highlight the flavors already present in the cocktail. If the bourbon has citrus notes, try citrus or fruity bitters. If the cocktail elements taste nutty and sweet, add spicy cinnamon or ginger bitters. Bitters have the power to drastically change the composition and balance of a cocktail. Take the time to taste-test the bitters you have (see chapter 2). The easiest test is to pour whiskey in a shot glass, add a drop or two of bitters, and see if they play well together. You can even re-create the bitters experiment for old-fashioneds in chapter 4's Cocktail Lab—this time for Manhattans.

> ## VERMOUTH-OF-THE-MONTH CLUB
>
> If you know a group of Manhattan fans, get together once a month to try different vermouths in Manhattans, Negronis, Boulevardiers, and other classic vermouth cocktails.

PLAY WITH THE SWEET VERMOUTH

Try a different brand or style of sweet vermouth. Because vermouths are infused with different botanicals, they can vary wildly. Experiment to find the one you love. Try French rouge vermouth if you're partial to sweet Italian vermouths. Branch out and try a dry vermouth in your Manhattan. Perhaps you might like a bit of Punt e Mes or Lillet Blanc to substitute for the sweet vermouth. As an experiment, omit the sweet vermouth and use a nontraditional flavor or liqueur as the third element in the cocktail.

PLAY WITH THE RATIO

To discover your perfect Manhattan, adjust the ratio—a little more whiskey to a little less vermouth, or a little more vermouth and bitters. You can even combine vermouths to blend the botanicals from two sources. Here are some common ratios to try in a Manhattan:

- 2 whiskey:1 vermouth

- 2.5 whiskey:0.5 vermouth

- 2 whiskey:0.75 vermouth

Setup for the Manhattan cocktail lab.

COCKTAIL LAB
VERMOUTH AND LIQUEUR EXPERIMENT

The best cocktails come from experimentation, and it's time to put on your cocktail lab coat! For this one, gather a mixing glass, stirrer, and strainer, along with rye, bourbon, sweet vermouth, dry vermouth, amaro, and bitters. You'll be making four versions of the Manhattan. To make this as scientific as possible, use the same whiskeys and bitters in each one so that you can taste the differences in the expressions.

1. Make a split-base Manhattan. Using the instructions for the classic Manhattan recipe given earlier, use 1 ounce rye, 1 ounce bourbon, 1 ounce sweet vermouth, and 3 dashes Angostura bitters. Strain into a serving glass and garnish. In a split-base Manhattan, you get pepper and spice from the rye, which balances well with the bourbon's sweetness. It might become your favorite iteration.

2. Make a Perfect Manhattan. In cocktails, *perfect* refers to a 50-50 split in an element. In this case, it means using half sweet vermouth and half dry. This variation is perfect for bourbon lovers who find the Manhattan too sweet. Using the instructions for the classic Manhattan, use 2 ounces bourbon, ½ ounce sweet vermouth, ½ ounce dry vermouth, and 3 dashes Angostura bitters. Strain into a serving glass and garnish.

3. Make a Reverse Manhattan. This version reverses the ratio of whiskey to vermouth. This cocktail's lower proof and enhanced botanical flavors make it perfect for people who enjoy gin- or wine-based cocktails. Using the instructions for the classic Manhattan, use 2 ounces sweet vermouth, 1 ounce bourbon, and 3 dashes Angostura bitters. Strain into a serving glass and garnish.

4. Make a Black Manhattan. This variation substitutes amaro for the sweet vermouth. Amaro is an infused bitter liqueur used as an after-dinner drink to improve digestion. The bittersweet amaro draws out completely different aromas and notes from the whiskey. Using the instructions for the classic Manhattan, use 2 ounces bourbon, 1 ounce amaro, and 2 dashes Angostura bitters. Strain into a serving glass and garnish.

Once you've sampled all the variations, compare and contrast them. Note which ones you love and which ones you don't. More important, figure out why you don't like some of them. Are they too floral? Too high proof? Are they too sour from the vermouth? This process helps you identify and refine your own aroma, flavor, and finish preferences.

Dos and Don'ts for Making a Manhattan

Do use a bourbon or whiskey you love. The whiskey is the star of the show. It's fine to use a whiskey that's not expensive, but choose one you enjoy drinking.

Do experiment with liqueurs and other wine-based products. Substitute a liqueur or port or sherry wine for the vermouth in a Manhattan. Try reducing the amount of whiskey and adding another flavor. Half an ounce of chocolate, nut, or cherry liqueur can change the tone and balance of the cocktail.

Do keep vermouth refrigerated. This keeps it fresh as you use up the bottle.

Do perform the sniff test for bitters. If you're not sure which bitters will work with the base spirits you're using, nose the whiskey and vermouth alongside the bitters choices. If they smell good together, chances are they'll make a great cocktail. But if they clash or compete, move on to another bitters.

Don't skimp on the garnish. Use fresh orange peel and high-quality cherries. Many people swear by Luxardo or Bada-Bing cherries. Be sure to express the oils from the orange peel over the cocktail before adding it to the glass.

Do chill the glass. Keep the coupe in the freezer or fill it with ice to chill while you make the cocktail. Because the Manhattan is served up (no ice), chilling the glass keeps the cocktail cold longer.

Espresso Manhattan

Use a whiskey with strong vanilla and caramel notes to simulate the taste of a fancy, high-proof latte. If you can't get the specific bitters called for in the recipe, experiment with any coffee and chocolate bitters you have on hand until you find the perfect balance.

1½ ounces midproof bourbon

½ ounce coffee liqueur (I use Patrón XO Café)

½ ounce sweet vermouth

½ ounce espresso, cold-brew, or any cold, strong coffee

5 drops Crude Big Bear coffee and cocoa bitters

1 dash Bitter Truth chocolate bitters

Garnish: coffee beans and orange peel

Combine ingredients in a mixing glass. Fill with ice and stir until chilled and well combined, about 30 seconds. Strain into a chilled coupe glass. Garnish with a few whole coffee beans and an orange peel. (See photo on page 28.)

Rosaline's Rebuff

I created this cocktail for a whiskey group called the BARDS (Bourbon and Rye Drinkers Society). It's based on a quote from Shakespeare's *Romeo and Juliet*: "What's in a name? That which we call a rose by any other name would smell as sweet." Rosaline is the woman Romeo was lusting after before the story starts. If he hadn't been rebuffed by Rosaline, his love story with Juliet never would have happened. I wanted to emphasize that love includes bitterness, so this cocktail had to be less about sweetness and more about balance (of love and fate). The Aperol, Chambord, and infused vermouth all give the drink a beautiful rose hue.

1 ounce Rittenhouse rye or high-rye bourbon

¾ ounce rose-infused dry vermouth (recipe to right)

¾ ounce Aperol

½ ounce Chambord black raspberry liqueur

3–5 drops rose water

Garnish: fresh raspberry or edible rose petal

Combine ingredients in a mixing glass, add ice, and stir for 30 seconds or until chilled. Strain into a chilled coupe glass and garnish.

Rose-Infused Dry Vermouth

1 cup dry vermouth

1½ tablespoons food-grade, organic dried rose petals

Combine vermouth and rose petals. Infuse for 1–2 days, depending on how much rose flavor you want in the vermouth.

Black Licorice Manhattan

If you love licorice or star anise, this cocktail is for you. It's wildly fragrant with licorice and spinning with citrus notes and chocolate earthiness. Every time I make this cocktail, I wish I'd made two. It's not a traditional Manhattan, but it's a balance of the flavors I love in my favorite bourbon expressions: citrus, chocolate, and licorice.

1½ ounces low- to midproof bourbon

½ ounce oleo saccharum

¾ ounce Ballotin chocolate whiskey (do not use a cream-based chocolate liqueur)

¼ ounce Copper & Kings absinthe

10 drops Woodford Reserve orange bitters

2 dashes Bitter Truth chocolate bitters

Garnish: orange wheel with star anise or chocolate shavings

Combine ingredients in a mixing glass and fill with ice. Stir for 30 seconds. Strain into a chilled coupe glass and garnish.

Black Licorice Manhattan.

Midnight Hour

It's time to get dark with my version of a Black Manhattan. It uses amaro, a bitter Italian digestif, paired with some autumn bitters to make a lovely dark drink to close out the fall.

2 ounces bourbon or rye whiskey (95–105 proof)

¼ ounce Carpano Antica sweet vermouth

¾ ounce Amaro Averna

8 drops Woodford Reserve sorghum and sassafras bitters

4 drops Bittermens Elekamule Tiki bitters

Garnish: lemon peel and cocktail cherry

Combine ingredients in a mixing glass and fill with ice. Stir until well chilled, about 30 seconds. Strain into a chilled coupe or martini glass and garnish.

Midnight Hour.

Drink Like a Girl.

Drink Like a Girl

My first sip of this cocktail was a revelation. Caramel and chocolate notes soar through the palate, and underneath is a solid foundation of great bourbon. This is a sweet after-dinner drink that's easy to put together and even easier to sip. It calls for a caramel liqueur, but make sure you use a noncreamy one (no Bailey's or cream liqueurs).

1½ ounces midproof bourbon
(I use 100-proof)

½ ounce Stroopwafel caramel liqueur
or other noncreamy caramel liqueur

½ ounce chocolate whiskey
or crème de cacao

2 dashes chocolate bitters

2 dashes aromatic bitters

Pinch of salt

Garnish: sea-salt caramel

Chill the glass. Pull a sea-salt caramel into a long string and drape it around the rim of the glass. Set aside. Combine ingredients in a mixing glass, add ice, and stir for about 30 seconds or until well chilled. Strain into the prepared glass.

Fleur-de-Lis Manhattan

Raspberry, bourbon, chocolate, and nut flavors take this Manhattan to the top of the list. It's an unpretentious, sweet variation—one to opt for *instead* of dessert.

1½ ounces 100-proof bourbon

¾ ounce Ballotin Bourbon Ball whiskey

¾ ounce Chambord black raspberry liqueur

3 drops Scrappy's cardamom bitters

2 dashes Scrappy's chocolate bitters

Garnish: grated chocolate, edible flowers, or ArtEatables chocolate truffle

Combine ingredients in a mixing glass, add ice, and stir for 30 seconds or until well chilled. Strain into a chilled coupe glass and garnish.

Fleur-de-Lis Manhattan.

Cask and You Shall Receive.

Cask and You Shall Receive (Barrel-Proof Manhattan)

Instead of loading the cocktail with bitters to balance the sweetness of the bourbon and the maple syrup, the coffee-infused vermouth provides balance and brings the elements together. This cocktail is designed for bourbon drinkers who prefer barrel-proof whiskey.

2 ounces barrel-proof bourbon (105–110 proof or higher)

¾ ounce coffee-infused sweet vermouth (recipe follows)

½ bar spoon maple syrup

4 drops Scrappy's cardamom bitters

8 drops orange bitters

Garnish: orange peel

Combine ingredients in a mixing glass, fill with ice, and stir until well chilled, about 30 seconds. Strain into a chilled coupe glass and garnish.

Coffee-Infused Sweet Vermouth

This infusion is also amazing in Negronis and Boulevardiers, and it makes an easy brunch spritz.

3 tablespoons dark-roast coffee beans

4 ounces sweet vermouth

Put coffee beans and vermouth in a clean glass jar. Steep for 8 hours or longer, up to 24 hours: the longer it steeps, the more bitter it becomes. Strain and store in the fridge in a clean jar. Use within 3–4 weeks.

Cocoa Manhattan

Bourbon and chocolate pairings are magical. This recipe combines chocolate liqueur and a bitter amaro (in place of vermouth) to make a chocolatey twist on the Manhattan.

2 ounces low- to midproof bourbon

½ ounce Ballotin chocolate whiskey or other dark chocolate liqueur (noncreamy)

½ ounce Meletti amaro

3 dashes chocolate bitters

3 dashes Woodford Reserve spiced cherry bitters

Garnish: cocoa; grated chocolate

Chill a coupe glass and dip the rim in cocoa. Combine ingredients in a mixing glass, fill with ice, and stir until well chilled, about 30 seconds. Strain into the chilled coupe glass and garnish with grated chocolate.

You Want a Peach of Me?

Peaches have both tart and sweet elements that play up the bourbon. A bit of Aperol balances the sweetness with some tart, bitter citrus oils.

1½ ounces 100-proof bourbon (smooth and nonaggressive)

1 ounce Giffard Pechê de Vigne peach liqueur

½ ounce Aperol

2 drops Herbsaint or absinthe (optional)

Garnish: orange peel and fresh peach

Combine ingredients in a mixing glass filled with ice. Stir until well chilled, about 30 seconds. Strain into a chilled coupe glass. Express the orange peel over the glass, rub the rim with the peel, and discard. Garnish with a fresh peach slice.

Eve's Pick

Lean into fall's apple and spice flavors with this double-infused Perfect Manhattan: dry vermouth infused with apples, and sweet vermouth infused with chai tea. This is a drink reminiscent of a chilly fall evening.

2 ounces bourbon

½ ounce apple-infused dry vermouth (recipe follows)

½ ounce chai tea–infused sweet vermouth (recipe follows)

2 dashes Bar Keep apple bitters

2 dashes Bittercube cherry bark vanilla bitters

Garnish: dried or fresh apple slice

Combine ingredients in a mixing glass and fill with ice. Stir until well chilled. Strain into a chilled coupe glass and garnish.

Chai Tea–Infused Sweet Vermouth

In a clean jar, place 1 herbal chai tea bag in 1 cup of sweet vermouth and infuse for 1 hour. Remove the tea bag and keep the vermouth refrigerated.

Apple-Infused Dry Vermouth

Add 1–2 chopped apples to a jar and top with dry vermouth. Refrigerate and infuse for 24–36 hours. Strain into a clean jar for use in Manhattans and martinis. Keep refrigerated.

Dark Quarter

If a Sazerac and a Manhattan had a love child, this would be their firstborn. Rich and complex, this cocktail dials up the spice with a licorice liqueur, a peppery rye whiskey, and amaro's earthy coffee and chocolate notes. A touch of maple syrup sweetens and balances the cocktail and results in a thicker mouthfeel.

2 ounces rye whiskey (or high-rye bourbon)

¼ ounce barrel-aged maple syrup

¾ ounce Foro amaro

¼ ounce Herbsaint or absinthe

Garnish: star anise and candied ginger

Combine ingredients in a mixing glass and add ice. Stir for 30 seconds or until well chilled. Strain into a chilled coupe glass and garnish.

HOW TO DESIGN YOUR OWN COCKTAIL (THE EASY WAY)

I frequently use this process to build cocktails when I have a specific flavor pairing or taste I want to re-create. I used this process for the Bananas Foster Manhattan in chapter 10.

1. Pick your flavors. You can base the cocktail on a food or whiskey pairing you love, a great meal you had, or a nostalgic flavor from your childhood—anything! (I chose Bananas Foster.)

2. Decide on a template cocktail: old-fashioned, toddy, Manhattan, whiskey sour, julep, and so on. Match the flavors to the cocktail, or vice versa.

(I chose a Manhattan because it's decadent and isn't served over ice, so it doesn't dilute.)

3. Swap some of the classic elements for the flavor profiles you want to add. (I dropped the vermouth and added banana liqueur, caramel liqueur, chocolate, and nut bitters.)

4. Test and refine.

Dark Quarter.

Legacy and Remembrance.

Legacy and Remembrance

This cocktail was originally designed for Uncle Nearest's 1856 Premium Whiskey—a Tennessee whiskey with apricot and nut notes—but you can use any balanced, fruity whiskey. In this cocktail, sage contributes a savory and bitter element. The Amaro Nonino adds bittersweet nut notes, helping the palate focus on the fruity tones.

1½ ounces Uncle Nearest's 1856 100-proof Premium Whiskey

½ ounce apricot liqueur (I recommend Giffard Abricot du Roussillon)

½ ounce Amaro Nonino

3 dashes Bittercube cherry bark vanilla bitters

Garnish: sage leaves and dried apricot

Rub the inside of a coupe or martini glass with a sage leaf until fragrant and place the glass in the freezer. Combine ingredients in a mixing glass and add ice. Stir until well chilled. Strain into the chilled glass and garnish with dried apricot and another sage leaf.

6 | THE WHISKEY SOUR

Bourbon and Citrus Steal the Show

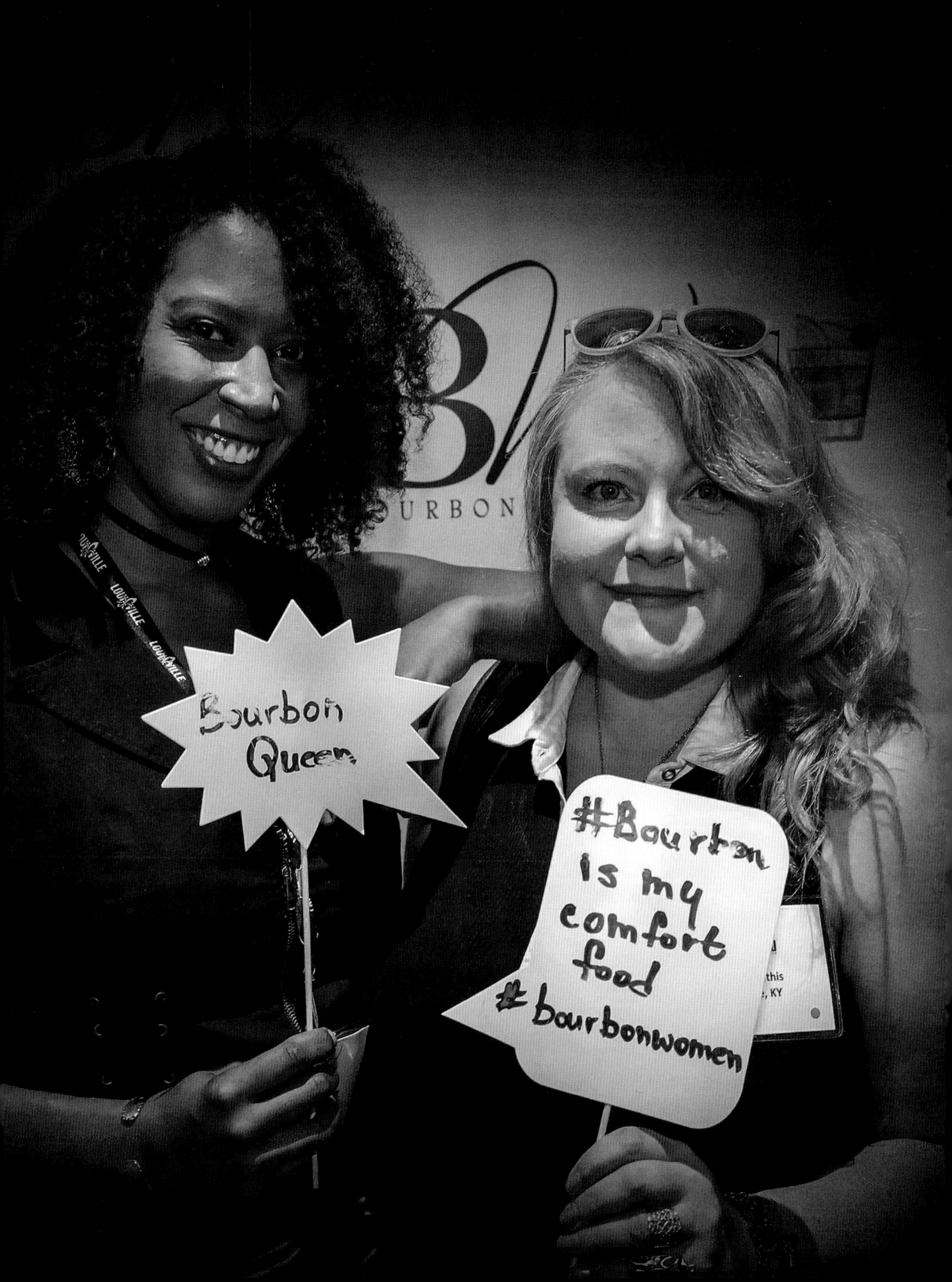
Bourbon Queen
#Bourbon is my comfort food #bourbonwomen

Curry Your Favor

This prize-winning recipe combines the flavors of apricot and lemon with the spice of a curry-infused simple syrup. Genius!

---

2 ounces Knob Creek
Small Batch bourbon

1 ounce fresh lemon juice

½ ounce madras curry–
infused simple syrup

¼ teaspoon apricot preserves

Garnish: apricot preserves and
curry powder; lemon wheel

Dip the rim of a coupe glass in apricot preserves and curry powder. Set aside. Add ingredients to a cocktail shaker over ice and shake. Strain into the prepared glass and garnish with a lemon wheel float.

By Jessica Samara, 2019 Bourbon Women "Not Your Pink Drink" professional winner

A summer staple, whiskey sours tickle the palate with their balance of sour citrus, sweet simple syrup, and whiskey burn. The variations on the classic sour are endless. I love to convert my guests into whiskey drinkers, and this cocktail delivers a whiskey finish in a tasty tipple.

The Nautical Origins of the Whiskey Sour

Like most whiskey classics, the sour has a long history. The first sours were created on sea voyages, as the citrus prevented sailors from succumbing to the scourge of scurvy on months-long voyages. Rum was watered down and combined with citrus, and a little sugar was added to make it more palatable. Sailors used rum because it was on hand (beer and wine often spoiled on long journeys), and the mixture was referred to as grog. There's nothing wrong with a cocktail as a daily supplement.

Over time, the medicinal tipple became a drink sailors liked, and they would look for it in port. In American ports, whiskey was more readily available, so it replaced rum. The first written mention of a whiskey sour is in Jerry Thomas's 1862 *Bar-Tender's Guide,* which described it as a combination of powdered white sugar dissolved in seltzer water, juice of half a lemon, and a couple ounces of bourbon or rye whiskey shaken with shaved ice and strained into a claret glass.

The Three Elements of a Whiskey Sour

The whiskey sour creates its magic with only three elements: whiskey, sugar, and citrus. The formula is easy to remember: two parts whiskey to one part sugar to one part citrus (sour). This ratio can always be tweaked according to the flavors you're using, but it's a good place to start.

Whiskey. Bourbon's vanilla, oak, and caramel notes tie in with the sugar used in the whiskey sour to create a sweet and mellow cocktail when the ratios are right. A midproof to high-proof bourbon soars through the sugar and citrus and contributes to a lovely finish. Lower-proof bourbons (80–90 proof) can be used, but the ratios should be adjusted to keep the whiskey from being overpowered. Lighter whiskeys match well when building cocktails with subtle floral or fruity notes. More aggressive flavors such as chocolate, baking spice, oak, and leather require a midproof bourbon to keep its flavor front and center, at least for those who want to taste the whiskey in their drink. Rye is another option in a whiskey sour. It contributes more pepper and spice to the cocktail's base, making it a better option for sours with more assertive flavors and citrus elements.

Sugar. The oldest recorded whiskey sours used powdered or granulated sugar to create a simple syrup in the glass before building the cocktail. Today, there are hundreds of choices for sweeteners, including honey syrup, maple syrup, molasses, and plain simple syrups. I prefer simple syrups for a consistent sweetness and mouthfeel in a whiskey sour. Any simple syrup can be used, but fruit- and spice-infused syrups add both sweetness and flavor. Substituting simple syrup with demerara, maple, or honey syrup drastically changes the flavor and highlights different notes in the whiskey. You can also substitute sweet-flavored liqueurs for all or part of the sugar. However, this will reduce the overall mouthfeel of the cocktail and can make it taste too thin.

Citrus. In food and flavor pairings, sweet and sour balance each other. If a dish or a drink is too sweet, adding sourness can restore balance, and vice versa. Lime works in some whiskey sours, but bourbon's flavor profile generally matches better with lemon. On its own, orange juice is too sweet and not acidic enough to balance the flavors of a whiskey sour, but pairing it with lemon juice creates a well-balanced cocktail.

Boston Sour.

Bitters (optional). Bitters aren't always used in whiskey sours, but they can enhance the aromatics and add flavor. A dash of aromatic, spice, or fruit bitters can add intrigue and interest to an otherwise flat sour, especially when those same aromatics are present in the drink's whiskey base. Like in the old-fashioned and the Manhattan, bitters round out the cocktail and tie it together.

The Three Whiskey Sour Styles

Whiskey sours are traditionally divided into three different styles: classic, Boston or Continental, and New York. Each brings different flavor combinations and balance to bear.

The classic whiskey sour—just whiskey, sugar, citrus, and perhaps some bitters—is built in a shaker and served in a rocks glass over ice. A perfect construction balances the three main elements in a refreshing tipple. The garnish is usually some combination of a lemon wheel and a cocktail cherry.

The Boston sour, also known as a Continental sour, includes egg whites or aquafaba (the juice from canned chickpeas) to create a creamy mouthfeel and a gorgeous head of foam. Bars serve Boston sours up in a chilled cocktail glass and garnished with fresh sprigs of herbs or patterned bitters droplets. Egg whites, aquafaba, and other foamers drastically change the mouthfeel and flavor balance of a whiskey sour. They tone down the burn of the whiskey and the pucker of the sour. As it's agitated, the foaming agent captures particles of air, much like when whipping a meringue. The cocktail feels creamy, soft, and luxurious in the mouth, and the foam creates a delightful canvas for fancy bitters, floral, or fresh herb garnishes.

> **Safety tip:** Don't be afraid of egg whites. For years, I didn't make whiskey sours with egg whites because I was afraid of salmonella. A single sip of a delicious craft cocktail changed that. To ensure safety, use pasteurized eggs, pasteurized egg whites in a carton, a vegan substitute such as aquafaba, or a cocktail foamer.

The New York sour is served with a red wine float on top of the cocktail. Although the classic recipe calls for a dry red wine, choosing a sweeter red wine or one with more or fewer tannic highlights contributes to the cocktail's overall taste and aromatics. Cabernet Sauvignon, Malbec, Merlot, or Shiraz wine adds a bit of tannic, dry sourness to the cocktail and a beautiful splash of red color.

Classic Whiskey Sour

2 ounces bourbon

¾ ounce fresh lemon juice

¾ ounce simple syrup

1–2 dashes bitters (optional; I use aromatic and black walnut bitters)

Garnish: lemon wheel and cocktail cherry

Add ingredients to a cocktail shaker. Fill with ice and shake vigorously for 10–12 seconds. Strain into a rocks glass filled with ice and garnish.

Boston Sour

2 ounces bourbon

¾ ounce fresh lemon juice

¾ ounce simple syrup

¾ ounce egg whites or aquafaba

Garnish: aromatic bitters

Add ingredients to a cocktail shaker with 1 or 2 large-format ice cubes. Shake vigorously for 30–60 seconds. Double-strain into a chilled coupe glass. Garnish with a few drops of bitters on top of the foam.

New York Sour

Note that a New York sour can be built on the base of a classic whiskey sour or a Boston sour.

2 ounces rye whiskey

¾ ounce fresh lemon juice

¾ ounce simple syrup

3 dashes aromatic bitters

½ ounce dry red wine

Garnish: lemon twist and cocktail cherry

Combine whiskey, lemon juice, simple syrup, and bitters in a cocktail shaker and fill with ice. Shake until very cold (10–12 seconds) and the outside of the shaker is almost too frigid to hold. Strain into a rocks glass filled with ice. Float the red wine on top of the cocktail using the back of a bar spoon. Garnish.

HOW TO MAKE AMAZING FOAM

There are all kinds of ways to create a gorgeous head of foam on a Boston sour, but my secret weapon is a handheld electric latte whisk. Put all the ingredients into a cocktail shaker, add ice, and shake for 10–15 seconds. Double-strain into another shaker or a mixing glass. To build up the foam, use the handheld latte whisk for 20 seconds. For the last 5–10 seconds, hold the whisk at a 45-degree angle to the surface of the cocktail, in the first inch of the liquid, to aerate the upper layers. Pour into a chilled coupe glass and garnish as desired.

New York Sour.

Making Your Own Riff on the Whiskey Sour

You can create endless variations by manipulating the flavors and elements of the classic whiskey sour. For example, use blackberry simple syrup, a little blackberry liqueur, and some black walnut bitters to transform the whiskey sour into a cocktail reminiscent of a blackberry cobbler (see the Sunset Sour recipe later in this chapter).

PLAY WITH THE CITRUS

Lemon juice is the most common sour element in the whiskey sour, but you can also use lime juice, grapefruit juice, orange juice (combined with lemon juice), or even a cocktail shrub (a syrup made from fresh fruits, sugar, and vinegar) or flavored vinegar. Combine two citruses—such as orange and lemon or lemon and lime—to match the other elements (syrup and whiskey). Always use fresh juices. They add a brightness that cannot be duplicated with canned or bottled juices.

PLAY WITH THE SYRUP

Syrups make a whiskey sour shine. An infused syrup—whether infused with fruit, spice, or something else—can either match or contrast the aromas and flavors of the whiskey. For example, using a vanilla simple syrup and a bourbon with baking spice flavors creates a heavenly sour. You can also add liqueurs to the cocktail to stand in for some of the syrup or some of the whiskey. Use a peach simple syrup with a little nut liqueur and some fruit bitters to create a perfect summer

> **Know your audience:** Perfecting the sour to please *your* palate is only half the battle. When you're creating cocktails for others, consider whether they prefer their sours on the sweet side or the sour side. For example, I love sours with a nice kick of pucker or bitterness, but if I'm mixing for my husband or family, I make the cocktail sweeter, without a big punch of sour.

> **Orange can't go it alone**. Although lemon and lime have similar levels of acidity, orange juice is much sweeter. To use orange juice in a sour, you need to add some lemon or lime juice to punch up the pucker. Although grapefruit juice is tarter than orange juice, it is also bitter, so it might need a little extra lemon as well. Always taste-test the elements of your cocktail.

sipper. Orange, cherry, fruit, spice, and bitter liqueurs like an amaro can build amazing flavor profiles. Syrups balance both sour and bitter elements in a cocktail; adding flavored or infused syrups can bridge the flavor differences between the base spirit and the other cocktail elements.

PLAY WITH THE RATIO

Although the classic whiskey sour ratio is 2:1:1, I prefer a ratio closer to 2 whiskey to ¾ sweet to ¾ sour. Depending on the sourness of the citrus juice, you might need to use a little more or less sweetener. For example, when using grapefruit juice with aggressive bitter notes, adjust the sweet element to achieve your preferred flavor ratio. Bitters balance both sweet and sour, so with a strong bitter element like an amaro, you might need more citrus or sweetness.

PLAY WITH THE SPIRITS

A fantastic whiskey sour keeps the whiskey flavor front and center to balance the sweet and sour elements. Among bourbon enthusiasts, bourbon is obviously their first choice, but any whiskey is acceptable in a whiskey sour. If the citrus and sweet flavors are very strong, mid-proof rye whiskeys have the spice and flavor to stand up to other loud elements. In such cases, using a split base of rye and bourbon or switching to all rye ensures that the whiskey is the star. When adding liqueurs or other spirits to a whiskey sour, consider reducing the amount of whiskey. Typical cocktails contain 1½ to 3 ounces of spirits.

Dos and Don'ts for Making a Whiskey Sour

Do use fresh citrus juice—always. Craft cocktail bars make lip-smacking whiskey sours because they use fresh juice. Although shelf-stable lemon juice is commonly available, it doesn't have the brightness or punch of fresh-squeezed juice. Always have a few lemons and limes on hand for fresh juice.

Don't overshake. Keep the shake short and vigorous, just 10 to 12 seconds (unless you're making a Boston sour). Shaking too long can over-dilute a cocktail. When making a Boston sour, shake longer to get a great foamy head (or use a handheld electric latte whisk), but be sure to use large, compact ice cubes that won't chip in the shaker.

Do experiment with liqueurs. Fruit and floral liqueurs taste amazing with the citrus element in a whiskey sour. Think of citrus-flavored drinks and dishes you like and pair them with those kinds of liqueurs. Peach, apricot, nut, and chocolate liqueurs can all sing in a sour. Try a bitter liqueur in a Boston or New York sour.

Don't fear egg whites. If you're worried about salmonella, use pasteurized eggs, egg whites in a carton, aquafaba, or a cocktail foaming agent. All these options introduce great creaminess and soften the flavors of the citrus and the spirit.

Do invest in a handheld latte whisk. For Boston sours, it's a game changer. Whisking for 20 seconds makes a luscious foam base for garnishes and bitters that will make your sour the envy of any bartender.

Do have fun with garnish. A fresh lemon wheel or cocktail cherry is traditional, but use your imagination. A few fresh berries, some nuts on a pick, or a sprig of herbs or flowers can dress up a sour for a fun night out.

Do chill the glass. If you're serving the sour up, chill the glass first to keep the cocktail cool while you sip it.

COCKTAIL LAB: WHISKEY SOUR EXPERIMENT

For this experiment, mix each of the three styles of whiskey sour using the same bourbon, ratio, and bitters. Although each variation is considered a whiskey sour, these are wildly different cocktails with different textures, flavors, and balance. This experiment allows you to gauge your preference for style, strength, mouthfeel, and flavor balance in the perfect sour.

1. Make a classic whiskey sour using a midproof bourbon, fresh lemon juice, and your favorite aromatic bitters. Follow the instructions for the classic whiskey sour recipe provided earlier. Serve over ice in a rocks glass and garnish.

2. Make a Boston sour using a midproof bourbon, fresh lemon juice, and a foaming agent. Egg whites are best, but you can use aquafaba or another foaming agent if you prefer. Follow the instructions for the Boston sour recipe provided earlier. Serve in a chilled coupe glass and garnish.

3. Make a New York sour using a midproof bourbon, fresh lemon juice, and a dry red wine float. Follow the instructions for the New York sour recipe provided earlier. Serve in a rocks glass over ice with a beautiful float and garnish.

4. Taste each variation and compare them. Note the difference in mouthfeel between the Boston sour and the other two. Note how the addition of the red wine float affects the aromatics and flavor of the New York sour. For each version, note how much of the whiskey comes through. Does the Boston sour or the New York sour need a higher-proof bourbon to keep the whiskey in the forefront? Do the sweet or sour elements need to be adjusted, based on the type of sour you're making?

Sunset Sour

In this gorgeous Boston-type sour, a touch of blackberry liqueur supports the blackberry cobbler notes from the simple syrup, and the black walnut bitters add a nutty note to balance the flavors. With just a blackberry as garnish, this cocktail looks as amazing as it tastes.

1½ ounces 100-proof bourbon

½ ounce blackberry liqueur

¾ ounce lemon juice

¾ ounce blackberry simple syrup (recipe follows)

¾ ounce egg whites or aquafaba (optional)

2 dashes Fee Brothers black walnut bitters

Garnish: fresh or frozen blackberries and lemon slice

Combine ingredients in a cocktail shaker and fill with ice. Shake vigorously for 10–12 seconds. Strain into a chilled coupe glass, or if you used the egg whites or aquafaba, strain into another shaker and use a handheld latte whisk for 20 seconds. Pour into a chilled coupe glass and garnish.

Blackberry Simple Syrup

2 cups frozen blackberries

½ cup water

1 cup sugar

Combine ingredients in a small saucepan and cook until the blackberries are thawed, soft, and very juicy. Once the blackberries have cooked down a bit, press on them to release the juice. Stir until the sugar is dissolved and the blackberries have turned purple. Cool and strain out the pulp. Store the syrup in the fridge, and save the strained blackberries to eat on ice cream.

Sunset Sour.

Too Fig to Fail Maple-Pear Sour

Fall's gorgeous flavors come to life in this easy Boston-type sour featuring pear brandy, barrel-aged maple syrup, and sassafras and sorghum bitters.

1½ ounces mid- to high-proof bourbon

½ ounce pear liqueur or brandy

½ ounce barrel-aged maple syrup

1 ounce lemon juice

1 egg white or ¾ ounce aquafaba

5 drops Woodford Reserve sassafras and sorghum bitters

Garnish: dark bitters

Combine ingredients in a cocktail shaker and fill with ice. Shake vigorously for 10–12 seconds. Strain into another shaker and use a handheld latte whisk for 20 seconds. Pour into a chilled coupe glass and use a cocktail pick to decorate the foam with drops of bitters.

Sugar Baby Sour

With this cocktail, summer refreshment is only a sip away. Sugar Babies are my favorite watermelons, and I designed this drink to taste like a great watermelon and mint salad. The bitters and optional peppercorn tincture add a slight savory note and a surprise on the finish.

2 ounces bourbon

1 ounce lemon juice

1 ounce watermelon simple syrup (recipe follows)

½ ounce egg whites or aquafaba (optional)

6 drops Crude Rizzo bitters (rosemary, grapefruit, peppercorn)

1 bar spoon peppercorn tincture (optional)

5 spanked mint leaves

Garnish: fresh watermelon and spanked mint leaves (optional)

Combine ingredients in a cocktail shaker and add ice. Shake for 10–12 seconds, until very cold. Strain into another shaker and use a handheld latte whisk for 20 seconds if using egg whites or aquafaba. Pour into a chilled coupe glass and garnish.

Watermelon Simple Syrup

1 pound watermelon, cubed

8 ounces sugar

Combine watermelon and sugar in a resealable bag and mix with your hands. Refrigerate for 24 hours. Strain out the chunks, and store the syrup in a glass jar in the fridge for 2–3 weeks.

Sugar Baby Sour.

Tarty Pants.

Tarty Pants

I originally called this cocktail Pants Optional because I created it shortly after the initial COVID-19 lockdown in Kentucky. In this drink, the grapefruit's bitter notes are amplified by the Campari, while the floral notes of the lavender engage with the bourbon's sweetness. (If you don't have lavender to make the simple syrup, honey syrup is an amazing substitute.) This is a great cocktail on a warm afternoon, especially when grapefruits are in season and you want a bitter, tart tipple.

2 ounces midproof bourbon

1 ounce fresh grapefruit juice

½ ounce fresh lemon juice

1 ounce lavender simple syrup (recipe follows) or honey syrup

½ ounce Campari

Garnish: grapefruit or lemon slices, sprig of lavender, or dried hibiscus

Combine ingredients in a cocktail shaker and fill with ice. Shake for 10–12 seconds. Double-strain into a rocks glass over ice and garnish.

Lavender Simple Syrup

2 tablespoons dried lavender

1 cup water

1 cup sugar

Boil water and pour over lavender. Steep for 10 minutes. Cool and strain. Add sugar and stir until combined. Store in the fridge for 2–3 weeks.

Lavender-Chocolate Sour

Some cocktails surprise you at the first sip. Here, dark chocolate notes and bright lemon flavors combine with lavender to create an intriguing and complex cocktail. Its layering of floral, earthy, and sweet flavors keeps it in the whiskey sour rotation year-round, not just in summer. I was inspired to create this cocktail by a tasting event in San Francisco where lavender chocolate was paired with a tart white wine.

2 ounces midproof bourbon

½ ounce lavender simple syrup (see recipe on page 119)

¾ ounce crème de cacao or noncreamy chocolate liqueur

¾ ounce lemon juice

¾ ounce aquafaba or egg whites

3 dashes chocolate bitters

Garnish: lemon peel and lavender sprig

Combine ingredients in a cocktail shaker. Fill with ice and shake for 10–12 seconds, until very cold. Strain into a second shaker or mixing glass and use a handheld latte whisk for 20 seconds. Pour into a chilled coupe glass and garnish.

HOW TO FIX A BROKEN COCKTAIL

It happens. Sometimes a cocktail doesn't turn out right. But don't panic. You can try a couple of quick fixes. If the flavor is off, add a small amount (¼–½ ounce) of a balancing element: if it's too sweet, add a little sour or bitter; if it's too bitter or too sour, add a little sweet. It doesn't always work, but it's worth a try before pouring the cocktail down the drain.

Lavender-Chocolate Sour.

Gimme the Peach!

Gimme the Peach!

Nothing says summer like fresh, juicy Georgia peaches. And the combination of flavors in this slightly smoky sour reminds me of all things summer. Top it with a raspberry popsicle, and eat the popsicle last, after it's fully infused with the smoke of the mezcal.

2 ounces peach-infused bourbon (infusion optional; recipe follows)

2 ounces peach-watermelon puree (recipe follows)

1 ounce lemon juice

½ ounce simple syrup

3 dashes Fee Brothers peach bitters

¼–½ ounce lightly smoked mezcal (optional, but highly recommended)

Garnish: raspberry popsicle and mint sprig

Combine ingredients in a cocktail shaker. Add ice and shake vigorously for 10–12 seconds. Double-strain into a large rocks glass filled with ice and garnish.

Peach-Infused Bourbon

Fill a quart jar with 2 cups of peeled, sliced peaches. Fill the jar with bourbon until it extends ½ inch over the top of the peaches. Infuse for 2 weeks, then strain and store in the fridge for up to 6 months.

Peach-Watermelon Puree

1 cup fresh sliced peaches

1 cup watermelon

½ ounce lemon juice

Combine peaches and watermelon in a blender and blend on high. Add lemon juice to help it retain its color. Like anything made with fresh peaches, this will slowly turn brown, so use it within a day or two.

Can You Fig It?

 This smoked honey and fig sour has a creamy mouthfeel and a gorgeous pink-orange color. It's like heaven in a glass. The secret ingredient is smoked chili bitters, which add a touch of smoke and heat. Note that this cocktail strains more slowly than other cocktails due to the seeds in the figs. Take your time—it's worth it.

3 quartered figs

½ ounce fall triple simple syrup (recipe follows)

2 ounces low- or midproof bourbon

3 dashes Hella Bitters smoked chili bitters

½ lemon, juiced

Garnish: fig

Muddle figs and simple syrup in a mixing tin. Add bourbon, bitters, and lemon juice and fill with ice. Shake for 10–12 seconds. Double-strain into a chilled coupe glass and garnish.

Fall Triple Simple Syrup

1 cup sugar

¼ cup brown sugar

¼ cup honey

1 cup water

¼ cup chopped peeled ginger

Combine ingredients in a small saucepan and simmer for 15 minutes. Turn off the heat and let the ginger steep in the syrup for 60 minutes. Strain into a clean jar and store in the fridge. This will keep for at least 3 weeks—longer if you add vodka to the mix.

Can You Fig It?

Whiskey Tiki Sour.

Whiskey Tiki Sour

Dress up a whiskey sour with orgeat (an almond-flavored syrup), some tiki-themed bitters, and pineapple juice for an extra splash of tropical flavor, and you've got a lovely cross between a whiskey sour and a tiki tipple.

2 ounces 100-proof bourbon or rye

¾ ounce orgeat (see note for substitution)

1 ounce pineapple juice

½ ounce lemon juice

20 drops Bittermens Elekamule Tiki bitters

Garnish: fresh or dried pineapple, mint, and cherries

Combine ingredients in a cocktail shaker. Fill with ice and shake for 10–12 seconds. Strain into a coupe glass or into a rocks glass over ice, depending on how fancy you want to be. Garnish with pineapple and mint if it's in season, and add a cherry or two if it suits you.

Note: If you don't have orgeat, use ½ ounce simple syrup, 1 bar spoon amaretto, and 1 bar spoon orange curaçao or another orange liqueur.

"One of the best Valentine's gifts my husband ever gave me, in fact, was a dozen 'Roses'—a bottle each of the Four Roses Yellow Label, Single Barrel, and Small Batch."

—Carla Carlton, former Bourbon Women board member

Everybody Hates Violet

This blueberry-cardamom sour is a gorgeous purple cocktail with a lovely balance of sweet, spice, and bitter. It combines peppery rye whiskey with a blueberry-cinnamon simple syrup and an herbal amaro for a fall-flavored sour.

1½ ounces rye whiskey or
high-rye bourbon

¾ ounce lemon juice

¾ ounce blueberry-cinnamon
simple syrup (recipe follows)

½ ounce Cardamaro or
other herbal amaro

8 drops Scrappy's cardamom bitters

1 egg white

Garnish: blueberries skewered
on a cinnamon stick

Combine ingredients in a cocktail shaker. Add ice and shake for 10–12 seconds. Strain into a mixing glass and use a handheld latte whisk for 20 seconds until thick and foamy. Pour into a chilled coupe glass or wine goblet and garnish.

Blueberry-Cinnamon Simple Syrup

2 cups blueberries

1½ cups sugar

½ cup water

4 cinnamon sticks

Simmer the ingredients until the blueberries start to break down and burst. Then turn off the heat and let the syrup cool. Strain through a fine metal sieve and store in a clean jar in the refrigerator for 2–4 weeks.

Everybody Hates Violet.

This One Goes to Eleven.

This One Goes to Eleven

This cocktail turns up the heat with a spicy kick provided by the pineapple serrano bitters and chili pepper flakes for garnish. It's a summer tipple that burns as soon as you stop sipping, so don't stop. Note that the inclusion of both lemon simple syrup and fresh lemon juice makes this a particularly sour drink. Adjust the lemon juice to suit your taste.

2 ounces midproof bourbon

½ ounce fresh lemon juice

1 ounce lemon simple syrup
(see recipe on page 75)

½ ounce orange liqueur (I used
Solerno blood orange liqueur)

¼ ounce Cynar, or your favorite amaro

2–3 dashes pineapple serrano bitters
or other moderately spicy bitters

Garnish: lemon wheel dusted
with chili pepper flakes

Combine ingredients in a cocktail shaker. Add ice and shake for 10–12 seconds. Double-strain into a chilled coupe glass and garnish.

Mandarin Orange–Fig Sour

In the dead of winter, when fresh fruit is not available, I use preserves or jams to sweeten my sours and anticipate the return of warm weather and balmy days. This fig-mandarin combination was so good I made it three days in a row. Don't use a regular navel orange, and don't peel the mandarin. Muddling the fruit with the peel on adds bitter orange oils to the cocktail—just what you need to balance the fig preserves and maple syrup.

1½ tablespoons fig preserves

1 mandarin orange *with peel,* chopped

2 dashes Crude Bitters Sycophant fig and orange bitters

1 dash Old Forester smoked cinnamon bitters

½ ounce lemon juice

¼ ounce chai simple syrup or maple syrup

2 ounces midproof rye or bourbon

1 egg white (optional)

Garnish: mandarin wheel and dried fig

Combine fig preserves, mandarin orange, bitters, lemon juice, and syrup in a cocktail shaker and muddle until the orange peels are fragrant. Add whiskey, egg white, and ice and shake for about 10 seconds. Double-strain into another shaker or a mixing glass and use a handheld latte whisk for 20 seconds to build the foam. Pour into a chilled coupe glass and garnish.

If there's one book I refer to over and over again when creating new cocktails, it's *The Flavor Bible: The Essential Guide to Culinary Creativity* by Andrew Dornenburg and Karen Page. They list foods, spices, and flavors, and for each entry they provide a subset of other foods that pair well with it—from apples to bacon and curry to cream. This is an invaluable source for compatible and unusual food pairings.

Peach-Rosemary Sour

Peaches and bourbon make a delectable cocktail, especially when you use a high-quality peach liqueur. In this one, the sweet and tart complexity of peach contrasts with a savory infusion of rosemary.

1½ ounces low- to midproof bourbon

½ ounce Giffard Pêche de Vigne peach liqueur

¾ ounce fresh lemon juice

¾ ounce peach-rosemary simple syrup (recipe follows)

8 drops Crude Bitters Rizzo (peach, magnolia, peppercorn)

¾ ounce egg whites or aquafaba

Garnish: sprig of rosemary, fresh peach slice, or lemon wheel

Combine ingredients in a cocktail shaker. Fill with ice and shake for 10–12 seconds, until very cold. Strain into another shaker or a mixing glass and use a handheld latte whisk for 20 seconds. Pour into a chilled coupe glass and garnish. (See photo on page 32.)

Peach-Rosemary Simple Syrup

This simple syrup is fabulous in everything from sours to juleps to old-fashioneds.

2 cups fresh or frozen peeled, sliced peaches

1 cup sugar

½ cup water

2 large sprigs rosemary

Combine ingredients in a small saucepan. Heat on low until the mixture is simmering. Cook for about 10 minutes, or until the peaches have released some of their juice and are breaking down. Remove from the heat and cool for about 30 minutes. Remove the rosemary and strain. Keeps in the fridge for 3–4 weeks.

Toast at the 2016 Bourbon Women
SIPosium. (Photo by Chris Joyce KY)

7 | HIGHBALLS, MULES, AND BUBBLY COCKTAILS

Bourbon Refreshment in a Tall Glass

American 46

An election season riff on the French 75, this cocktail uses Borough bourbon made by Republic Restoratives Distillery in Washington, DC, the nation's largest women-owned, crowd-funded distillery. Using honey syrup instead of simple syrup allows the honey and bourbon to blend together to sweeten the dry bubbles used to top the cocktail. When the lemon zest is expressed over the surface, the lemon oils and honey create a great flavor contrast with the dry champagne.

2 ounces Borough bourbon

¾ ounce honey syrup

¾ ounce fresh lemon juice

2–4 ounces sparkling wine

Garnish: lemon zest

Shake bourbon, syrup, and lemon juice with ice for 10–12 seconds. Strain into a champagne flute. Top with sparkling wine as your mood dictates, and garnish.

Washington, DC, branch of Bourbon Women—submitted by Republic Restoratives Distillery

The simplest of all cocktails is the highball: just whiskey and soda. While the earliest iterations called for plain soda as the carbonated ingredient, today, ginger ale or one of the hundreds of flavored carbonated beverages can be used. An unflavored soda or seltzer allows the bourbon to shine, but a flavored soda allows you to pair notes from the whiskey. Imagine a highball with a pour of Old Forester 1920, with its cherry notes, topped with a cherry pomegranate Pellegrino.

The mule, a descendant of the highball, consists of a spirit, a dash of citrus (usually lime), and ginger beer. The splash of lime juice and the spicy bite of the ginger beer create a more complex cocktail when the base spirit is whiskey. Commonly called a Kentucky mule when bourbon is used, this is a refreshing summer cocktail for hot afternoons. Kentucky mules, other bourbon cocktails made with carbonated beverages, and champagne cocktails are grouped together in this chapter because of their similarity to the highball.

The Original Two-Ingredient Cocktail

The highball was first recorded in print just before the turn of the twentieth century. In the late 1890s, Chris Lawlor described a "High Ball" in *The Mixicologist* as a drink served in an ale glass with ice, seltzer, and a float of half a jigger of brandy or whiskey. The highball may have come to the United States from Britain, where a drink consisting of soda and brandy was experiencing a surge in popularity. Given the rise of Scotch whisky in the 1800s, it's likely that the

> ### PROFESSIONAL TIP
> Keep all the elements frosty! This ensures that the cocktail will stay bubbly and carbonated throughout consumption. And make sure the glass is well chilled too.

> ### PROFESSIONAL TIP
> When mixing highballs for a bourbon-centric crowd, keep the proof high and the soda flavor low. When hosting a party, batch the highball ingredients, except for the soda, before the guests arrive. Then simply pour the batched ingredients over ice, top with soda or bubbles, and garnish with a lemon wheel or herb sprig.

Scottish were the first to experiment with whiskey in their soda. As carbonated drinks and ice became more available, both were put to good use in the cocktail.

The classic highball is a "built" cocktail, meaning that it's made in the glass it's served in. After adding the carbonated element, it's important to stir only once to keep the bubbles from rushing out of the cocktail with each swirl.

The Two (or Three) Elements of a Highball

The beauty of a highball is its simplicity. Beyond the two key elements—whiskey and soda—you can experiment by adding citrus or other mixers, such as flavored liqueurs or syrups, to build a flavor palate for a tall, cold, carbonated drink. Another important consideration is the texture of a highball. Think about how a cold carbonated beverage feels on the tongue. It pops and crackles in the mouth, giving the liquid a texture different from the silky smoothness of a Manhattan. Carbonation changes the mouthfeel in a textured, random way.

Whiskey. With only two main ingredients, the whiskey matters. I tend to use a mid- or high-proof bourbon in highballs because of the volume of the drink and because I want to taste the whiskey in each sip. When crafting for those who prefer a lighter whiskey burn, dial down the proof of the bourbon and choose whiskeys with less aggressive flavor profiles (wheated bourbons are an excellent option).

Soda. Choose high-quality brands of ginger ale and ginger beer, and look for companies that specialize in cocktail mixers such as Fever-Tree, Q Mixers, or Regatta Craft Mixers. Though slightly more expensive, mixers specifically designed for cocktails keep the drink's ingredients from being overwhelmed by sugary sodas. Use unsweetened seltzers or sodas to add flavor without increasing the overall sweetness of the drink.

Citrus. Always use fresh citrus juice for any mule or highball variation. But note that using a citrus peel accentuates the aromatics of the citrus as you consume the cocktail. Lemon is more common in a highball, and lime is traditionally associated with the Kentucky mule.

Whiskey Highball

2 ounces bourbon

4–6 ounces soda or ginger ale

Garnish: lemon wedge or twist

Fill a chilled highball glass with ice and add bourbon and soda. Give the glass one quick swirl with a bar spoon and garnish.

Kentucky Mule

2 ounces low- to midproof bourbon

½ ounce fresh lime juice

Ginger beer to top

Garnish: lime wheel and mint sprig

Combine bourbon and lime juice in a copper mule mug. Stir briefly, fill with cracked or pellet ice, and top with ginger beer. Garnish.

Practice What You Peach Highball
(see page 142).

Making Your Own Riff on the Highball or Kentucky Mule

Although the traditional highball has just two ingredients, this chapter covers other cocktails with a fizzy element, so there are a few more variables to tweak when creating your own version of the classic cocktail.

> **Sniff test:**
> To match mixers with whiskeys, put a small amount of soda in a glass and nose it with the whiskey options. If they smell great together, chances are the flavors will be a great match as well.

PLAY WITH THE WHISKEY

Any good whiskey can build a great highball. Experiment by combining different whiskeys and spirits to create a flavor base. A split base can be as simple as combining bourbon and rye, or it can be made more complex by replacing part of the whiskey with rum, sherry, or aged tequila. Adding a bit of smoke with peated whiskeys or mezcal works here because of the larger volume of a highball. The smoky notes dilute and offer merely a suggestion of smokiness rather than a punch in the face.

PLAY WITH THE SODA

Swapping out the ginger beer in a Kentucky mule for tonic water gives you a bourbon and tonic—delicious and refreshing on a hot summer day. Experiment with flavored seltzers such as watermelon, cherry, tangerine, or pomegranate. You can even start with a soda and pick a whiskey to match.

ADD FLAVORS VIA SPIRITS AND SYRUPS

To add complexity to the basic highball, try a splash of citrus, a flavored liqueur, or a simple syrup. Layer the flavors to create a more complex, balanced drink. For example, to create a winter highball, match a high-proof, aggressive whiskey with a chai tea simple syrup and cinnamon bitters, and top with ginger ale. Or tweak the cocktail with summer flavors: a bit of fresh lemon or pineapple, an orange liqueur, or a fresh raspberry garnish. Adding Italian bitter liqueurs to a highball makes the cocktail more complex. As the ice melts, the drink dilutes, bringing different flavors to the fore. A highball leans closer to a spritz in a delightful way with the addition of amaro and a topping of bubbles.

PLAY WITH THE RATIO

Highball recipes have mixer-to-whiskey ratios of 2:1 to 4:1. If a highball recipe doesn't have the whiskey balance you want, adjust the ratio up or down to suit your taste.

FOR MULES, PLAY WITH THE CITRUS

Lime is traditional in a Kentucky mule, but you can experiment with lemon or even grapefruit. With lemon, you might be able to use nut or spice liqueurs. With grapefruit, a little extra sweetness from a liqueur or a bittersweet amaro can tone down the grapefruit's bitterness. Both flavors mutate in pleasant ways over ice in a highball. But remember to always use fresh citrus.

FOR SPARKLING COCKTAILS, PLAY WITH THE BUBBLES

Just as bourbons have hundreds of flavor profiles, so do sparkling wines. There are myriad classifications of champagnes, proseccos, cavas, and more. Any highball can be matched with sparkling wines instead of soda to add a wine-flavored kick.

The highball's extended family includes the Seven & Seven, rum and Coke, Tom Collins, John Collins, mimosa, Paloma, gin and tonic, and spritz. They all embrace the simplicity of a spirit and a carbonated beverage. And one of the easiest ways to play with highballs is to taste them as you build them.

Setup for the highball cocktail lab.

Dos and Don'ts for Making a Whiskey Highball

Do chill the glass beforehand. The key to a fabulous highball is a very cold glass and very cold soda. Together, they slow the release of carbonation, keeping the drink effervescent and bubbly from the first sip to the last.

Don't overstir. A quick stir of the bar spoon around the edges of the glass starts the mixing process, which is completed by the action of the bubbles as they are released and travel to the surface.

Do use large blocks of ice. Using a few large ice cubes instead of pellet, cracked, or refrigerator ice keeps the drink bubbly and reduces the dilution effect as the ice melts.

Do experiment with garnish. Try adding fruit, fresh herbs, or spices to the glass. This gives the drink visual interest and affects the nose and taste of the highball.

Don't limit yourself to just two ingredients. To add more flavors and aromas to a highball, add a splash of citrus, a touch of liqueur, some simple syrups, or even bitters. When using more than one extra ingredient, consider mixing all the nonsoda ingredients first and then pouring them into the highball glass. This avoids overstirring after the soda is added.

Practice What You Peach Highball

This is a perfect highball for the height of summer. It improves on the basic highball with a peach liqueur, spicy bitters, and a hint of aromatics from the garnish. If you prefer a drier drink, use unflavored seltzer instead of ginger ale.

2 ounces bourbon or rye

½ ounce Giffard Crème
de Pêche de Vigne

8 drops Crude Bitters Lindsay
(pecan, magnolia, habanero)

Frozen peaches (optional)

4 ounces ginger ale or
unflavored seltzer or soda

Garnish: basil or mint sprig,
fresh peach slice

Add whiskey, peach liqueur, and bitters to a highball glass. Stir briefly. Add ice and frozen peaches (if using frozen peaches, add them intermittently between ice cubes). Top with ginger ale and stir one last time. Spank the mint or basil lightly and add it to the glass with a peach slice.

COCKTAIL LAB:
BOURBON HIGHBALL EXPERIMENT

Because highballs are made right in the glass, experimenting is a snap. Here, you'll start with two basic highballs and add elements, tasting as you go to see how the cocktail changes as more flavors are added. For example, note how the whiskey interacts with the sour elements and bitters.

1. In a chilled highball glass, add 2 ounces bourbon, ice, and cold soda water. Leave some room at the top, as you'll be adding a few extra elements. Give the cocktail a quick stir, then take a sip or two. Note the flavor of the whiskey and soda alone.

2. Add ½ ounce lemon juice, give it a quick swirl, and take another sip. Note how the addition of the citrus changes the taste of the bourbon and the balance of the cocktail. It's probably too sour at this point.

3. Add ½ ounce flavored simple syrup—something lightly floral or fruity, such as blackberry, peach, or lavender simple syrup. The syrup balances the tartness of the lemon juice and can also tie in to the bourbon's fruity notes, which are more prevalent when it's diluted. You now have a cocktail closer to a John Collins.

4. In a clean, chilled highball glass, add 2 ounces bourbon, ice, and ginger ale. Again, leave some room at the top. Give the cocktail a quick stir, then take a taste. Note how the flavor of this cocktail differs from the one made with soda. I often get more baking spices from a highball made with ginger ale or ginger beer.

5. Add ½ ounce of a liqueur. I recommend an orange or nut liqueur. Liqueurs add both sweetness and alcohol to the drink. Taste the cocktail and notice how the liqueur adds to the flavor.

6. Add ½–1 ounce of a bitter amaro: Averna, Campari, and Montenegro are all excellent choices. The bitter liqueur balances the sweetness of both the other liqueur and the ginger ale. Adding bitters often makes the whiskey flavor more pronounced and sets off some of the more subdued flavors from the liqueurs and sodas.

Bourbon-Campari Highball.

Bourbon-Campari Highball

I love the combination of a great amaro and bourbon, and I wanted to create a highball that celebrates how well bitters and bourbon work together. Taking a nod from the classic Italian spritz cocktail, this high-proof highball uses a bit of Campari and Cardamaro.

1½ ounces bourbon, 100 proof or higher (add an extra ½ ounce if it's missing that whiskey zing, or use a higher-proof whiskey)

½ ounce Campari

2 bar spoons Cardamaro

4–6 ounces Fever-Tree spiced orange ginger ale

Garnish: orange peel or wheel

In a highball glass, add ice and pour in bourbon, Campari, and Cardamaro. Give it a quick stir. Top with ginger ale, give it one more quick stir, and add garnish.

DESIGNING A PHOTOWORTHY GARNISH

To wow friends and followers with the beauty of your cocktail experiments, here are a few tips:

- Add a garnish that's a bright or contrasting color.

- Match the garnish shape with the glass type. For highball glasses, use long curls, tall herb sprigs, or pineapple leaves to accentuate height. For coupe glasses, use twists, curls, single-leaf garnishes, or a skewer of berries or cherries to follow the shape of the bowl.

- Use directional lighting. Take a photograph near a window or in a dark room with the light to the left or right side instead of overhead. Turn off any extraneous lights.

Lavender-Citrus Highball

A green whiskey cocktail always comes as a shock to me, but this flavor combination is a keeper. Lavender and citrus always make a great whiskey cocktail, but the blue curaçao gives the drink a fun vibe and a vibrant green color.

1½ ounces bourbon (use 2 ounces if you like more of a whiskey kick)

½ ounce lavender simple syrup (see recipe on page 119)

¼ ounce blue curaçao (or other noncolored orange liqueur for a less colorful highball)

4–6 ounces San Pellegrino Aranciato orange sparkling water

Garnish: orange rose and lavender sprig

In a highball glass, add bourbon, lavender simple syrup, and blue curaçao and stir lightly a few times. Fill with ice, top with orange sparkling water, and stir one more time. Garnish.

Proof's Up Pomegranate Highball

Stepping back from the sweet, this dry highball magnifies the flavors of a great bourbon with cherry notes (I used Old Forester 1920). This dry, refreshing cocktail is perfect for the whiskey drinker who doesn't thrive on sweetness.

1½ ounces mid- to high-proof bourbon with cherry notes

1 ounce pomegranate juice

3 dashes cherry bitters

4–6 ounces pomegranate cherry Pellegrino

Garnish: pomegranate arils or cocktail cherry

Combine bourbon, pomegranate juice, and bitters in a chilled highball glass. Stir briefly, add ice, top with Pellegrino, and stir one more time. Garnish.

Lavender-Citrus Highball.

Blackberry-Cardamom Mule.

PROFESSIONAL TIP

I often photograph mules in a glass to showcase the beautiful colors, but to stay true to the spirit of the cocktail, use a copper mug. While it doesn't affect the flavor, the metal mug keeps the drink frigid and well carbonated.

Blackberry-Cardamom Mule

Blackberry and ginger play well together, but pairing them with a dash of lime juice and a hint of cardamom creates a complex yet easy-to-build cocktail. The color gradient makes this drink as fun to look at as it is to sip. I use a nutty bourbon rather than one with mostly caramel notes. I mix the ingredients in a mixing glass, but feel free to build this cocktail right in the mug.

1½ ounces low- or midproof bourbon

½ ounce fresh lime juice

½ ounce blackberry simple syrup (see recipe on page 114)

1–2 dashes Scrappy's cardamom bitters

4–6 ounces ginger beer

Garnish: fresh or frozen blackberries, lime wheel, and candied ginger (optional)

Combine bourbon, lime juice, simple syrup, and bitters in a mixing glass. Add ice and stir for 10 seconds. Strain into a copper mule mug filled with crushed or pellet ice. Top with ginger beer. Garnish.

> "There is a long history of women as distillers and as whiskey drinkers. You don't need any gender-specific body parts to enjoy bourbon or other whiskeys. Everyone appreciates great flavors and elegant, well-made sippage, be it wine, beer, or whiskey."
>
> —Susan Reigler, Bourbon Women president, 2015–2017

Watermelon Mule

Summer sings with this bright and tasty variation on the basic Kentucky mule. Enjoy it while spending the afternoon at the pool.

2 ounces bourbon

½ ounce fresh lime juice

½ ounce watermelon simple syrup (see recipe on page 116)

4–6 ounces ginger beer

Frozen watermelon cubes (optional)

Garnish: watermelon cubes, fresh mint

Combine bourbon, lime juice, and simple syrup in the bottom of a copper mule mug. Stir briefly, add crushed or pellet ice, and top with ginger beer. Use frozen watermelon cubes to replace some of the ice for additional flavor. Garnish.

Hibiscus-Ginger Highball

This gorgeous red highball packs a lemony, ginger punch—perfect for an afternoon at the beach or relaxing in a hammock.

2 ounces Rittenhouse rye (or any high-proof rye)

½ ounce hibiscus-ginger simple syrup (recipe follows)

8 drops Meyer lemon bitters

2 dashes Hella Bitters ginger bitters

2–4 ounces hibiscus-lemongrass sparkling beverage

Garnish: candied ginger and dried sweetened hibiscus flowers

Combine rye, simple syrup, and bitters in the bottom of a highball glass. Stir. Add ice to the glass, top with a sparkling beverage, and give it one last swirl. Garnish.

Hibiscus-Ginger Simple Syrup

½ tablespoon dried hibiscus flowers

1 cup water

1 cup sugar

1½ inches peeled ginger root, minced

Heat water to a boil. Add dried hibiscus flowers. Steep for 8 minutes. Strain and transfer to a small saucepan. Add sugar and ginger root. Bring to a boil and simmer for about 5 minutes. Turn off the heat and steep for 60 minutes. Strain and refrigerate. Store in the fridge for 2–4 weeks.

Hibiscus-Ginger Highball.

Bubbles and Bourbon

It may not be a formal cocktail category, but the combination of bourbon and bubbles creates a refreshing and elegant cocktail with a nice kick. A wine float on a New York sour adds both flavor and aroma components, and so does a champagne or sparkling wine float. I'm a huge proponent of adding prosecco or sparkling wine to the top of cocktails. I love to see what happens to the flavor. Sparkling wines can also be substituted for sodas in any highball-type recipe.

Old-Fashioned Bubbles

This easy recipe is based on an old-fashioned and adds a sparkling wine float. Here, I started with my favorite recipe for an old-fashioned, but any one will do. Simply cut the ingredients in half and top with champagne.

1 ounce low- to midproof bourbon

¼ ounce brown sugar simple syrup

1 dash aromatic bitters

1 dash orange bitters

Champagne or sparkling wine

Garnish: cocktail cherry, orange peel

Combine bourbon, simple syrup, and bitters in a mixing glass. Add ice and stir until chilled, about 30 seconds. Strain into a champagne flute and top with sparkling wine. Garnish.

Any cocktail can be elevated with a sparkling wine topper. It makes even the simplest cocktails taste more complex and look fabulous. Simply split a normal-sized cocktail between two chilled coupe glasses and top with a sparkling wine that matches a flavor element in the cocktail.

Call to Post

The bugle call before each race at Churchill Downs in Louisville sends chills of excitement down any Kentuckian's spine—especially on the first weekend in May. The deep red hue of the hibiscus simple syrup recalls the beautiful dresses and hats women wear at the racetrack.

1 ounce bourbon

½ ounce hibiscus simple syrup (recipe follows)

¼ ounce Solerno blood orange liqueur

Champagne

Garnish: destemmed cherry

In a mixing glass, combine bourbon, simple syrup, and liqueur. Add ice and stir until well chilled, about 20 seconds. Strain into a champagne flute and top with champagne. Garnish.

Hibiscus Simple Syrup

½ tablespoon dried hibiscus flowers

1 cup water

1 cup sugar

Heat water to a boil. Add dried hibiscus flowers. Steep for 8 minutes. Strain. Add sugar and stir until dissolved. Store in a clean glass jar in the refrigerator for 2–4 weeks.

When There Are Nine

Asked when there would be enough women on the Supreme Court, the notorious Ruth Bader Ginsburg (RBG) famously replied, "When there are nine." In her honor, I created a sparkling wine cocktail that is light and fruity as well as tart and spicy. I think RBG would approve.

1 ounce passionfruit juice

1½ ounces Rowan's Creek bourbon

½ ounce ginger liqueur

½ ounce simple syrup

1 bar spoon Cardamaro (or any amaro with baking spice notes)

½ dropper Old Forester hummingbird bitters

Sparkling wine

Garnish: candied ginger

Combine passionfruit juice, bourbon, ginger liqueur, simple syrup, amaro, and bitters in a mixing glass. Add ice and stir until well chilled. Strain into a champagne flute or coupe glass and top with sparkling wine. Garnish.

When There Are Nine.

Bourbon Women event at the Frazier History Museum, 2016. (Photo by Chris Joyce KY)

8 | THE JULEP

More than a Drink at the Racetrack

Frozen Mint Julep

Susan Reigler and Joy Perrine's *The Kentucky Bourbon Cocktail Book* set the standard. In the early days of Bourbon Women's "Not Your Pink Drink" contest, Joy mixed the recipes submitted for the judges to evaluate. Her frozen version of the mint julep is easy to make and great for a crowd (with a cup of bourbon, this recipe should make 3–4 frozen juleps).

1 cup Kentucky bourbon

½ cup Kentucky mint simple syrup (recipe follows)

¼ cup mint leaves

Garnish: fresh mint sprigs

Place ingredients in a blender. Add ice to fill. Blend. Pour into cups or glasses and garnish.

Kentucky Mint Simple Syrup

1 cup water

1 cup Kentucky Colonel mint leaves

1 cup cane sugar

Boil water and add mint leaves. Boil 2 minutes. Add sugar and boil 1 minute. Cover and remove from heat. Steep at least 6 hours or overnight. Strain, bottle, and refrigerate. Keeps approximately 1 week.

By Joy Perrine, Kentucky Bourbon Hall of Fame, Bourbon Women founding member

The julep is a cocktail consisting of spirits and sugar served over crushed ice with a fresh herb garnish, and the variations are endless. Although it's a storied cocktail with a mysterious history, for many bourbon lovers, the mint julep is underwhelming. But with a little care in the ingredients and construction, it can turn into a summer favorite.

For Kentuckians, the mint julep is associated with fond memories of the Kentucky Derby: watching with a frosty julep in hand as the horses thunder down the stretch toward the finish line. I grow small plots of mint so I'll have two or three varieties to choose from, and if I'm lucky, I've got a healthy crop of mint by the first weekend in May and the running of the Kentucky Derby.

More than any other bourbon cocktail, the mint julep is not just a drink: it's an experience. It's the frosty cup that's so cold you have to hold it by the rim; the waft of mint and bourbon rising together from the drink's surface; the tickle of the generous mint garnish on your nose as you sip; the ice-cold temperature of the drink in your mouth. The combination of taste, smell, and touch creates a sense memory that other cocktails can only dream of.

History of the Mint Julep

The history of the julep goes back much further than that of other cocktails. The word *julep* comes from the Persian *gulab* and the Arabic *julab*, both of which refer to a sweetened drink made from rose water. This drink traveled to medieval Europe via the trade routes, and for hundreds of years, Europeans used the word *julep* to refer to medicines or tinctures sweetened with syrup to make them more palatable. By the time Americans created the mint julep, the name may have been a tongue-in-cheek reference to a medicinal whiskey tipple to start the day.

It's not a julep without the ice! Therefore, the modern julep didn't exist until the early 1800s, when the Industrial Revolution made the harvesting, shipping, and storage of ice a commercial reality. The earliest mint juleps were likely made with brandy or rum, as these were the most common spirits among the upper class at the time. Since then, bourbon has become the standard when making a julep.

Because mint juleps were popularized in the South, many believe that they were first crafted by enslaved people on plantations. One of the most famous julep makers in the United States in the 1800s was an emancipated African American man named Cato Alexander. Another famous African American bartender was John Dabney, who worked at the Sweet Springs resort in West Virginia and made juleps for the guests. Both men are recognized as important personalities associated with the popularity of juleps in the South.

The Four Elements of a Julep

Whiskey, sugar, ice, and herb: that's all you need to make a julep. It's a simple cocktail, but choosing quality ingredients for each element vastly improves the outcome.

Whiskey. It's traditional to use bourbon, and although you can select a different spirit base, I start all my julep experiments with either bourbon or rye. Because the cocktail is served over crushed ice, it dilutes quickly, so choose a mid- to high-proof whiskey.

Sugar. Some build a mint julep in a glass with granulated or powdered sugar, but I prefer simple syrup. The syrup doesn't pulverize the mint leaves as much as sugar does during the muddling process, and it mixes with the rest of the drink more easily and consistently.

Ice. Unlike most other cocktails, the julep requires a specific kind of ice. If you don't use crushed or pebble ice, you won't get the slick, frosty effect on the exterior of the cup—a central facet of the julep experience.

Herb. A traditional julep gets its freshness from a sprig of mint, but any fresh herb can be used as a garnish. Basil, especially cinnamon or lemon basil varieties, can be fantastic in a julep. Wintry juleps might use rosemary or sage, and a sprig of thyme can introduce wonderful savory notes. Whatever herb garnish you use, it must be fresh and fragrant, and it must be spanked.

Classic Mint Julep

2 ounces bourbon

½ ounce simple syrup

10 mint leaves

Garnish: fresh mint sprig

Take 1 mint leaf and rub it inside the julep cup, especially around the rim. Add simple syrup and the remaining mint leaves and muddle lightly. Add bourbon. Fill with ice and stir once or twice to combine. Top with more ice if there's room. Garnish with a mint sprig and add a straw right next to it.

JULEPS AND THE DERBY

By the late 1800s, the julep's popularity was firmly entrenched at US racetracks. During Prohibition, journalists lamented the loss of the mint julep at horse-racing venues. In 1939 the mint julep became the official drink of the Kentucky Derby, and today, more than 120,000 are served on Derby Day.

Making Your Own Riff on the Mint Julep

One of the beautiful things about a mint julep is that it's so easy to vary in interesting and flavorful ways. Creative combinations of garnishes and simple syrups can make bold statements and can highlight more subtle flavors and aromas in the drink.

PLAY WITH THE SPIRIT BASE

Select a mid- to high-proof bourbon or whiskey. I love to use bottled in bond bourbons at 100 proof because the whiskey doesn't get lost when diluted by the crushed ice. But experimenting with rum, brandy, rye, or even some flavored whiskeys can yield intriguing results.

PLAY WITH THE SWEETENER

Rather than a simple syrup or demerara syrup, use fruit syrups or infused syrups to create layers of flavor. For example, one of my favorites is a blackberry-basil julep with a touch of blackberry simple syrup and a fresh sprig of basil. When creating juleps for the fall, consider using vanilla or cinnamon-maple simple syrup with a mint garnish and perhaps a fan of fresh apple slices.

PLAY WITH THE HERB

Juleps rely on the garnish more than other classic bourbon cocktails do. The julep experience depends on aromatic cues from the herb as you sip, so the garnish is integral. Swapping out the herbs is a fast and easy way to test combinations. Although mint is traditional, basil is a fun substitute. By midsummer, fresh basil is everywhere, and its heady aroma paired with berries or stone fruit and whiskey packs a lovely punch. Floral herbs such as lavender, bee balm, rosebud, jasmine, chamomile, and lemon balm can also be used as garnish in a julep. Savory herbs such as sage, rosemary, fennel, thyme, marjoram, tarra-

PROFESSIONAL TIP

The julep is served with a straw, which should be tucked right next to the garnish. This draws your lips and nose close to the aromatic herbs. If the straw is more than 1½ inches higher than the top of the garnish, trim it. The garnish should tickle the nose with each sip.

Mint juleps.

Classic Mint Julep.

PROFESSIONAL TIP

Take a leaf or sprig of the herb
garnish and rub the inside of
the julep cup, especially the rim.
This transfers fragrant oils to the
interior and edge of the glass,
enhancing the herb's presence
as you sip the cocktail.

gon, cilantro, and dill can be surprisingly good when paired with a grassy or herbal whiskey and a fruit or berry syrup. Sometimes I build a cocktail based on whatever garnish is flourishing in the garden. To test the pairing of an herb and a whiskey, pour a sample of the whiskey into a tasting glass and nose it along with the herb to determine whether the aromas complement each other.

PLAY WITH BITTERS OR LIQUEURS

Although bitters and liqueurs are not traditional in juleps, bitters can correct a julep with an overly sweet flavor profile, and liqueurs can broaden the flavor combinations in a julep. I love to use chocolate flavors in a julep. A chocolate-mint julep might remind you of your favorite cookie (see the recipe on page 177), and the combination of chocolate and peanut butter can make a tasty julep. I sometimes add peach, apricot, banana, or ginger liqueur to juleps to highlight the flavors in the bourbon.

Dos and Don'ts for Making a Mint Julep

Do use a metal julep cup. Some photographs depict juleps in a glass to showcase the color,

COCKTAIL LAB: JULEP EXPERIMENT WITH AROMATIC HERBS AND SYRUPS

This cocktail lab walks you through some basic pairings of herbs and syrups to help you develop a julep version you love. For this experiment, you'll be making five different juleps, and you'll need maple syrup, honey syrup, and three fresh herbs: mint, basil, and rosemary. (If you have other syrups you want to play with, substitute those instead.)

1. Mint-honey julep: Prepare the julep cup by rubbing mint leaves on the inside. Then build the julep by muddling ½ ounce honey syrup and 8 mint leaves; add 2 ounces bourbon, crushed ice, and a mint sprig.

2. Mint-maple julep: Prepare the julep cup by rubbing mint leaves on the inside. Then build the julep by muddling ¼ ounce maple syrup and 8 mint leaves; add 2 ounces bourbon, crushed ice, and a mint sprig. Note the flavor difference when using maple syrup versus honey syrup. Do you prefer one over the other?

3. Honey-basil julep: Prepare the julep cup by rubbing basil leaves on the inside. Then build the julep by muddling ½ ounce honey syrup and 6 large basil leaves; add 2 ounces bourbon, crushed ice, and a basil sprig.

4. Honey-rosemary julep: Prepare the julep cup by rubbing a rosemary sprig on the inside. Then build the julep by muddling ½ ounce honey syrup and 1 large sprig of rosemary; add 2 ounces bourbon, crushed ice, and a rosemary sprig. Compare the flavors of the two different herb garnishes. Is one more savory than the other? Does one pairing work better with the bourbon you're using?

5. Wild-card julep: Devise your own combination of syrups and herbs, and build the julep as you did for the other versions.

As you taste the different juleps, note how the different garnishes affect not just the smell but also the taste of the drink. This is because most flavor perception comes from the nose. Aromatics drive taste, as this experiment proves.

but if I'm serving a julep for drinking, I always choose a metal julep cup.

Do use crushed or pellet ice. The combination of crushed ice, alcohol, and a metal cup creates an icy frost on the outside of the julep cup. This can't happen if you use ice cubes.

Don't forget the straw. Tuck the straw right next to the garnish to make sure that each sip includes the aromatics of the fresh herb.

Do poke a hole through the crushed ice for the garnish. If the mint sprig can't cut through the ice, use the straw to create a hole big enough to accommodate both the garnish and the straw.

Don't skimp on the garnish. Whether you're using fresh mint, basil, rosemary, or thyme, be generous. The scent wafting from the herb gar-

nish ensures that each sip is infused with those fresh aromatics.

Do spank the herbs. Before placing the herb garnish in the julep cup, spank or slap it against the back of your hand. This slight bruising dramatically increases the scent of the garnish.

Don't overmuddle the herbs. When working with delicate herbs such as mint or basil, muddle them lightly. Vigorous muddling turns them bitter and leaves tiny pieces of shredded herb in the cocktail.

Do underdilute. Because you're using crushed or pebble ice, underdilute slightly when using a mixing glass or when building the cocktail in the julep cup.

Dawn at the Downs

 With coffee, maple, and orange flavors, this breakfast julep is a perfect way to start Derby Day or any day. If you want to add a little bacon too, have at it! Convert ounces to cups to expand this recipe to serve 8.

½ ounce coffee liqueur

¼ ounce orange liqueur

½ ounce maple syrup

8 mint leaves

2 ounces bourbon

Garnish: fresh mint sprig

Rub 1 mint leaf on the inside and rim of a julep cup. Add liqueurs, maple syrup, and remaining mint leaves and muddle lightly. Add bourbon and give everything a quick swirl. Fill the cup with crushed ice and clear a small hole for the garnish and straw. Spank the mint sprig and add as garnish.

Dawn at the Downs.

Triple Crown Pie Julep.

Triple Crown Pie Julep

A favorite dessert at Derby parties is bourbon-spiked chocolate pecan pie. This julep is Kentucky's favorite pie in a metal cup.

1½ ounces midproof bourbon

¾ ounce Rivulet pecan liqueur

¾ ounce Ballotin chocolate whiskey or crème de cacao

3 dashes chocolate bitters

Garnish: fresh mint sprig

Fill a julep cup with crushed ice. In a mixing glass or cocktail shaker, combine ingredients, fill with ice, and stir 10–15 seconds. Strain into the julep cup. Spank the mint sprig and slide it into the cocktail next to the straw.

Blackberry-Basil Julep

Blackberries are both sweet and tart, so using them to make a simple syrup is a decadent way to take advantage of a bountiful harvest and flavor all kinds of cocktails from the old-fashioned to the sour to the julep. For a more licorice-like flavor, use Thai basil instead of sweet basil in the syrup. No blackberries? Try strawberries, blueberries, or raspberries—they all make fantastic infusions with basil.

2 ounces bourbon

½ ounce blackberry-basil simple syrup (see recipe on page 72)

½ ounce blackberry liqueur

4 basil leaves

Garnish: sprig of fresh basil or lemon verbena

In a mixing glass, combine ingredients and muddle basil just a bit. Add ice and stir until well chilled, about 20 seconds. Strain into a julep cup filled with crushed ice and add garnish.

The King's Julep

Here, the King refers to the King of Rock and Roll: Elvis Presley. This julep is an homage to those peanut butter and banana sandwiches Elvis used to make. It's a great julep for someone who is new to bourbon and wants to try a wildly creative take on a classic.

1½ ounces bourbon

¾ ounce peanut butter whiskey

¾ ounce Giffard Banane du Brèsil banana liqueur (or substitute chocolate liqueur for a Reese's julep)

2 dashes Bittercube cherry bark vanilla bitters

Garnish: peanut butter and banana skewer and fresh mint sprig

In a mixing glass, add ingredients and ice. Stir until chilled, 10–15 seconds. Strain into a julep cup filled with crushed ice. Add a straw, mint sprig, and skewer of banana and peanut butter.

Peach, Please Julep

Whether peaches are served fresh over vanilla ice cream or baked into a warm cobbler, they always go well with bourbon. For this julep, I paired peaches with basil, but mint would work equally well.

"Women have been a part of the industry for more than 200 years; we just didn't get credit for it. Today, things are changing for us."

–Peggy Noe Stevens, founder, Bourbon Women

2 ounces bourbon

½ ounce peach simple syrup (recipe follows)

½ ounce peach liqueur

5 basil leaves

Garnish: sprig of fresh basil

Rub 1 basil leaf on the inside and rim of a julep cup and pack the cup with crushed ice. In a mixing glass, add simple syrup, peach liqueur, and remaining basil leaves and muddle lightly. Add bourbon and fill the mixing glass with ice. Stir until well chilled, 10–15 seconds. Strain into the julep cup. Spank the basil garnish and put it right next to the straw.

Peach Simple Syrup

2 cups peeled, chopped peaches

2 cups sugar

Combine peaches and sugar in a resealable plastic bag and muddle until well mixed. Leave the bag in the fridge overnight (or up to 24 hours), until the peaches have expressed most of their juice and most of the sugar is dissolved. Strain and store in the fridge in a clean glass jar for 3–4 weeks.

The King's Julep.

Ginger-Chai Julep

If you're looking for a julep with a little more spice, this delicious and refreshing version is the one for you. The fall flavors make it a perfect julep to serve on cool autumn evenings.

1½ ounces midproof bourbon

½ ounce ginger liqueur

½ ounce chai simple syrup
(recipe follows)

8–10 mint leaves

Garnish: 2 fresh mint sprigs,
cinnamon stick, star anise

Rub 1 mint leaf on the inside and rim of a julep cup and pack it with crushed ice. In a mixing glass, combine bourbon, ginger liqueur, simple syrup, and remaining mint leaves and muddle lightly. Add ice and stir 10–15 seconds. Strain into the julep cup. Spank the mint sprig before adding as garnish.

Chai Simple Syrup

1 cup strongly brewed chai
tea (2–3 tea bags)

1 cup sugar

Combine warm chai tea and sugar in a jar and shake until dissolved. Store in the fridge.

PROFESSIONAL TIP

With most bourbons, it's easier to detect caramel, vanilla, and oak notes than herbal notes. But one way to help your nose is to gather fresh herbs from the garden or from the farmer's market and use them when selecting a bourbon for a julep. Hold the sprig near the mouth of the tasting vessel as you nose it. Sometimes smelling mint, sage, or lemon balm helps you detect that note in the bourbon.

Ginger-Chai Julep.

Starlight Strawberry Julep.

Starlight Strawberry Julep

Huber's, an orchard in Starlight, Indiana, is my go-to place for fresh strawberries, and luckily, they're plentiful right around Derby Day. For this julep, mint or basil can be substituted for the lavender in the simple syrup or as garnish.

2 ounces midproof bourbon

1 large strawberry, chopped

1 sprig fresh lavender

8 drops Scrappy's lavender bitters

1 ounce strawberry-lavender simple syrup (recipe follows)

Garnish: sprig of fresh lavender, fresh strawberry

Add the strawberry, lavender, and bitters to the bottom of the mixing glass and muddle briefly. Add bourbon and simple syrup. Add ice and stir for 15 seconds. Strain into a julep cup filled with crushed ice. Garnish.

Strawberry-Lavender Simple Syrup

1½ cups strawberries, pureed and strained

1 cup sugar

½ cup water

1 tablespoon dried lavender

Simmer water, sugar, and strawberry puree for 2–3 minutes on low heat until the sugar dissolves. Add lavender, turn off the heat, and let it steep for 20–30 minutes. Strain the syrup and cool completely before use. Store in a clean glass jar in the fridge for 2–3 weeks.

Caramel Brûlée Julep

A favorite pairing of mine is salted caramel and bourbon. Bourbon often sings with notes of caramel, vanilla, and brown sugar, so to bump up the wow factor, I included a bit of vanilla simple syrup and a whipped cream topping. This is more dessert than cocktail, so purists may gasp (but the kid in them will be secretly pleased). Note that your more bourbon-centric friends might prefer a stronger ratio of bourbon to caramel, so adjust as needed.

2 ounces 100-proof bourbon

½ ounce salted caramel syrup (the type added to coffee)

¼ ounce vanilla simple syrup (recipe follows)

2 dashes chocolate bitters

Garnish: fresh mint sprig, whipped cream, salted caramel, kosher salt

Combine ingredients in a mixing glass and fill with ice. Stir until well combined but slightly underdiluted, about 15 seconds. Strain into a julep cup, fill with crushed ice, and top with whipped cream, a drizzle of salted caramel, a sprinkle of kosher salt, and a spanked mint sprig.

Vanilla Simple Syrup

Make simple syrup as usual (see chapter 2), but cut open a vanilla bean and add the inner beans and the whole pod to the syrup. Steep for 1 hour. This syrup is also a fine addition to old-fashioneds and whiskey sours.

Cocktail trivia:
The paper straw was invented for the julep. They were called Stone's Patent Paper Julep Straws and were accompanied by a note stating, "One straw necessary for each drink." Earlier straws were made of natural products such as hay, which added flavor to the drink. Stone must have loved his juleps.

Caramel Brûlée Julep.

Desert Rose Julep.

Desert Rose Julep

Given the julep's Persian origins as sweetened rose water, I created a drink with flavors from that time and place. Stone fruits always match well with bourbon, so here I chose apricot to pair with the honey and rose flavors.

½ ounce rose-honey simple syrup (recipe follows)

2 dashes rose water (optional)

8–10 mint leaves

1½ ounces bourbon

½ ounce Giffard apricot liqueur

Garnish: fresh mint sprig, dried apricots, organic food-safe rose petals

Add simple syrup and rose water to the bottom of a mixing glass. Tear mint leaves in half and drop them into the syrup. Muddle lightly. Add bourbon and apricot liqueur. Fill with ice and stir until chilled and well combined but underdiluted, about 15 seconds. Strain into a julep cup filled with crushed ice and garnish.

Rose-Honey Simple Syrup

2 tablespoons dried rosebuds

1 cup water

¾ cup honey

Brew rosebuds in boiling water for 8 minutes, like tea (I use a teapot to do this). Strain ½ cup into a measuring cup and, while still hot, add honey and stir well to combine. Cool completely and store in the fridge in a clean glass jar.

Chocolate-Mint Julep

One of my favorite pairings is chocolate and mint. This recipe celebrates that combination in an easy and fun cocktail. In spring, you may be able to find this flavor combination in cookie form from the Girl Scouts.

1½ ounces low- to midproof bourbon

1½ ounces Ballotin chocolate mint whiskey

15 drops Scrappy's chocolate bitters

8–10 mint leaves

Garnish: fresh mint sprig, chocolate mint cookie

Rub the inside of a julep cup with 1 or 2 mint leaves and discard them. Add bourbon, whiskey, bitters, and remaining mint leaves to a mixing glass and muddle briefly. Add ice. Stir until well chilled, 15–20 seconds. Strain into the prepared julep cup, fill with crushed ice, and add garnish and a paper straw.

Toast at the 2016 Bourbon Women SIPosium's
opening-night dinner. (Photo by Chris Joyce KY)

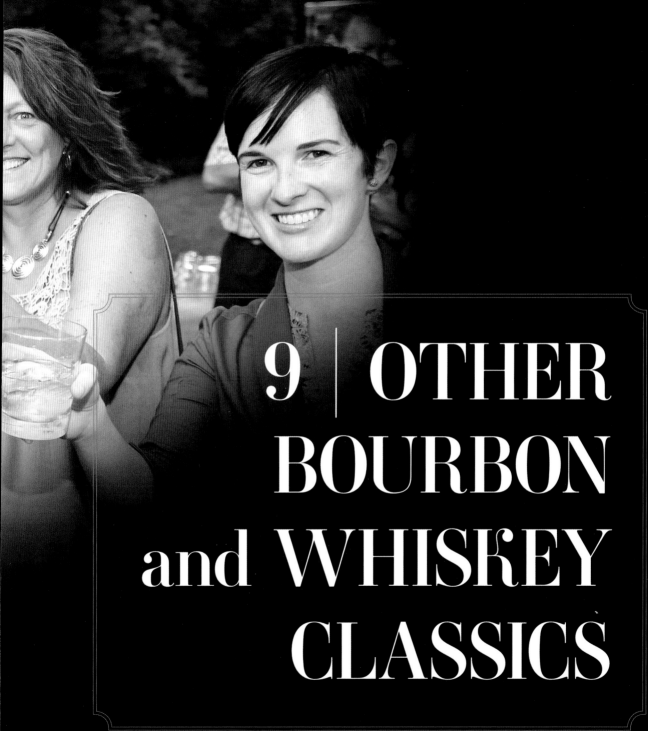

9 | OTHER BOURBON and WHISKEY CLASSICS

Bourbon Sling

This elegant bourbon sling by Bobby Ridenour of Rivue Restaurant and Lounge combines the flavors of bourbon, lemon, and orange served up in a martini glass.

2 ounces Basil Hayden bourbon

1 ounce Cointreau

Lemon juice, freshly squeezed, from 1 whole lemon

1 ounce simple syrup

Garnish: Maraschino cherry

Fill shaker ¾ full of ice. Add ingredients and shake vigorously 20 times. Strain into a martini glass. Garnish.

By Bobby Ridenour, 2013 "Not Your Pink Drink" professional winner

C lassic whiskey cocktails come in all shapes and sizes, and I could devote an entire chapter to each one. Here, I present variations on the Sazerac, whiskey smash, Boulevardier, and hot toddy—all favorites of bourbon enthusiasts.

Sazerac

Legend has it that the Sazerac was born at the Sazerac Coffee House in New Orleans in the mid-1800s. Its name comes from a French brandy called Sazerac-de-Forge et Fils, a popular spirit in New Orleans at the time. When a grape blight decimated the harvest in Europe, Americans switched to rye whiskey, giving us the modern version—a classic rye whiskey cocktail with simple syrup, Peychaud's bitters, and an absinthe rinse. (One theory even posits that pharmacist Antoine Peychaud created the drink to boost sales of his medicinal bitters. Then, when Peychaud sold his store to Thomas Handy, Handy took the recipe, bottled it, and made it famous.)

However, some cocktail historians dispute this origin and suggest that the original Sazerac was developed and recorded later, in the 1890s, as a form of the Improved Whiskey Cocktail famous in other parts of the country. The earliest written evidence of a Sazerac cocktail is in an 1899 Alpha Tau Omega journal discussing a convention held the year prior. By 1900, the cocktail was associated with the Sazerac House bar and had become one of the top cocktails in the country. Although the origins of the cocktail's ingredients (with or without the Sazerac name) likely date from the mid-nineteenth century, the Sazerac's name and popularity can be pinpointed to the turn of the century.

The Sazerac is usually served neat with an expressed lemon peel in a chilled rocks glass that has been rinsed with absinthe. The easiest way to control the amount of absinthe is to put it in a small atomizer and mist the inside of the glass before pouring in the drink.

Like its cousin the old-fashioned, the Sazerac can be tweaked by adding different liqueurs, bitters, and infused spirits. With just four elements—rye whiskey, simple syrup, bitters, and an absinthe rinse—the easiest variations involve altering the simple syrup and the bitters. Common variations split the base between rye and cognac or swap out another aromatic liqueur, such as Fernet, for the absinthe.

Classic Sazerac

2 ounces rye whiskey (or high-rye bourbon)

½ ounce simple syrup

3 dashes Peychaud's bitters

¼ ounce absinthe (for rinse)

Garnish: lemon peel

Rinse or mist a chilled rocks glass with absinthe and set aside. Combine whiskey, simple syrup, and bitters in a mixing glass and add ice. Stir until well chilled, about 30 seconds. Strain into the prepared rocks glass and express a lemon peel over the surface.

Chocolate Sazerac

If you love the taste of chocolate and licorice together, you'll love this take on a classic Sazerac. The cooling sensation of the absinthe paired with the sweet and bitter flavors of chocolate will surprise and delight you—if you're an absinthe lover. Avoid using creamy chocolate liqueurs.

2 ounces rye whiskey (or high-rye bourbon)

¼ ounce simple syrup

¼ ounce crème de cacao (or Ballotin chocolate whiskey)

2 dashes Peychaud's bitters

2 dashes Scrappy's chocolate bitters

Absinthe rinse or mist

Garnish: orange peel

Rinse a rocks glass with absinthe and place it in the freezer. Combine whiskey, simple syrup, crème de cacao, and bitters in a mixing glass and add ice. Stir until well chilled, about 30 seconds. Strain into the chilled rocks glass. Express an orange peel over the cocktail and attach it to the rim if you like.

Sazerac Slushie

This frozen cocktail, along with the absinthe, has a cooling effect on the tongue. It's easy to prepare in advance and delicious served right out of the freezer. A large quantity of lemonade is needed to drop the alcohol level enough for the drink to freeze.

2 ounces 100-proof rye or high-rye bourbon

¾ ounce simple syrup

6 dashes Peychaud's bitters

7 ounces lemonade

¼–½ ounce absinthe (100 proof)

Garnish: lemon peel rose or wheel, fresh mint sprig, spritz of Peychaud's bitters or absinthe (optional)

Combine ingredients in a small container and place in the freezer for at least 8 hours but preferably overnight. When ready to serve, remove from the freezer, lightly flake the cocktail, and add a spritz of bitters to the top. Serve in a chilled glass with garnish.

Chocolate Sazerac.

Sazerac Slushie.

Batch of 8–10 Sazerac Slushies

2 cups whiskey

¾ cup simple syrup

20–30 dashes Peychaud's bitters

7 cups lemonade

¼–⅓ cup absinthe

Follow the instructions for a single slushie (see page 182), but be sure to chill overnight.

Whiskey Smash

The classic whiskey smash is the love child of the julep and the whiskey sour—a combination of muddled fruit, citrus, herbs, sugar, and (occasionally) bitters, plus whiskey. Some pour the whiskey smash into a rocks glass, muddled fruit and all, while others strain the cocktail into an ice-filled rocks glass for a more refined presentation. Either way, the taste is fantastic.

When building variations on the smash, mix and match fresh herbs and fresh fruit (seasonal is best) for fun combinations such as peach-basil, apricot–lemon thyme, or raspberry-mint. A walk through the farmer's market can be your best inspiration for a smash. You can also use frozen fruit, but it must be thawed first. Because it's easy to overmuddle delicate herbs like mint and basil, muddle the fruit, citrus, and hardier herbs first, then add the delicate herbs for a final light muddling.

PROFESSIONAL TIP

One of the secrets to making a great whiskey smash is to muddle fresh citrus with the peel on. This supplies bitter citrus notes, eliminating the need to add aromatic or flavoring bitters (unless you want to).

Classic Whiskey Smash

½ lemon, quartered

1 ounce simple syrup

8–10 mint leaves

2 ounces whiskey

Garnish: fresh mint sprig, lemon wheel

Place lemon and simple syrup in the bottom of a shaker. Muddle to release the lemon juice. Add mint leaves and muddle lightly just 2 or 3 times. Add whiskey, fill with ice, and shake vigorously for 10–12 seconds, or until the outside of the shaker is almost too cold to hold. Strain into a rocks glass filled with ice and garnish.

Pineapple-Peach Smash

This cocktail is a celebration of the summer tastes of pineapple, peach, and basil. The unaged whiskey provides a more herbaceous, young whiskey flavor.

½ ounce peach simple syrup (see recipe on page 168)

3 peach slices

3 pineapple chunks

5 basil leaves

1 ounce midproof bourbon

½ ounce unaged whiskey or unflavored moonshine

½ ounce Giffard Crème de Pêche de Vigne peach liqueur

¾ ounce lemon juice

¼ ounce St. Elizabeth allspice dram (optional)

Garnish: basil, peach wedges, pineapple

Combine simple syrup, peaches, and pineapple in the bottom of a mixing tin and muddle until the fruit juices have been released. Add basil and muddle again briefly. Add whiskeys, peach liqueur, lemon juice, and allspice dram. Fill with ice and shake until very cold, 10–12 seconds. Strain (or not) into an ice-filled rocks glass and garnish.

Blackberry-Sage Smash

Blackberries combine beautifully with the savory aromatics of sage. Here I use orange instead of lemon because fresh blackberries already have a tart kick. (See photo on page 34.)

5 large blackberries

1 slice orange

1 ounce blackberry simple syrup (see recipe on page 114)

5 sage leaves

½ ounce blackberry liqueur

2 ounces midproof bourbon or rye whiskey

Garnish: sage sprig, blackberries

Combine blackberries and orange in the bottom of a shaking tin, add simple syrup, and muddle to press the juices from the berries. Add sage leaves and muddle lightly again. Add blackberry liqueur and whiskey. Add ice and shake vigorously for 10–12 seconds. Rub a sage leaf around the rim of a rocks glass, fill it with ice, and strain the smash into the glass. Garnish.

Pineapple-Peach Smash.

Boulevardier

Today, the Negroni is more popular than the Boulevardier, but the Boulevardier recipe was published long before the Negroni name was tied to it. The original Boulevardier was a simple cocktail with just three ingredients—equal parts bourbon, sweet vermouth, and Campari. It was developed by Erskine Gwynne, an American expatriate and founder of a gentlemen's magazine in Paris called *Boulevardier*. It was first recorded in Harry McElhone's *Barflies and Cocktails* in 1927. Bourbon lovers often tweak the original ratio, adding slightly more bourbon to keep the sweet vermouth and Campari from overpowering the drink.

Given the limited number of ingredients, it might seem like there's not much room for variation, but in addition to increasing the ratio of bourbon, you can create a Campari infusion and use that in a Boulevardier (see chapter 3 for tips on spirit infusions). You can even substitute different red bitters or amaro to make things more interesting. So get out your lab coat and start experimenting.

Classic Boulevardier

1½ ounces bourbon

¾ ounce sweet vermouth

¾ ounce Campari

Garnish: orange peel

Combine ingredients in a mixing glass and fill with ice. Stir until well combined, about 30 seconds. Strain into a chilled rocks glass with one large-format ice cube and garnish with an expressed orange peel.

Coffee Boulevardier

Adding coffee to Campari (an Italian bitter liqueur) gives it an earthiness that combines beautifully with its citrus notes. This simple recipe has a punch of coffee flavor that makes the cocktail richer and more complex.

1½ ounces 100-proof bourbon

¾ ounce sweet vermouth, Carpano Antica Formula

¾ ounce coffee-infused Campari (recipe to right)

Garnish: orange peel, coffee beans

Combine ingredients in a mixing glass and add ice. Stir until well chilled, about 30 seconds. Strain into a chilled rocks glass with one large-format ice cube and garnish.

Coffee-Infused Campari

3 tablespoons dark-roast coffee beans, cracked slightly with a muddler

1 cup Campari

Place coffee beans and Campari in a jar for up to 1 day. Check the infusion every 4–8 hours until you're satisfied with the flavor. For a darker, more bitter espresso flavor, infuse longer or use darker-roast beans. Strain and store in a clean glass jar in the fridge for 1–2 months.

Coffee Boulevardier.

Chocolate-Covered Strawberry Boulevardier

There's something magical about strawberry-infused Campari. When it's combined with chocolate liqueur, chocolate bitters, and a bit of sweet vermouth, the result is a fabulous dessert cocktail for bourbon lovers and Boulevardier fans.

1¼ ounces bourbon

1 ounce sweet vermouth

¼ ounce crème de cacao

¾ ounce strawberry-infused Campari

3 dashes chocolate bitters

Garnish: strawberry, mint sprig, chocolate square

Combine ingredients in a mixing glass and add ice. Stir until well combined, about 30 seconds. Strain into a chilled rocks glass with a large-format ice cube and garnish.

Felicia's Bully Boulie

This recipe comes from Felicia Corbett, mixologist extraordinaire, assistant beverage director at Trouble Bar, and Bourbon Women board member. She infuses sweet vermouth with a chocolate pu'erh tea she gets from a local tea shop: Sis Got Tea. And instead of relying on Campari, she opts for a lighter and sweeter Aperol, letting the chocolate and tea notes burst through. Though Felicia doesn't specify a type of whiskey, this combination would be exquisite with either bourbon or rye.

1½ ounces whiskey

1 ounce Aperol

1 ounce chocolate pu'erh tea–infused sweet vermouth (recipe follows)

Garnish: orange swath

Combine ingredients in a mixing glass and fill with ice. Stir until well chilled, about 30 seconds. Strain into either a rocks glass with one large-format ice cube or a coupe glass and garnish.

Chocolate Pu'erh Tea–Infused Sweet Vermouth

Infuse sweet vermouth with chocolate pu'erh tea for up to 1 day at room temperature. When pleased with the flavor, strain the tea infusion and store in the fridge.

Hot Toddies and Warm Cocktails

Bourbon works wonders in cocktails of all temperatures, but in a hot drink like a toddy or a boozy hot chocolate, its vanilla and caramel notes soar and combine in delicious ways. In a warm drink, the flavors of the alcohol are accentuated, so you can use less whiskey in a bigger cocktail and still get that warm bourbon hug after each sip.

At its simplest, a toddy consists of hot water, lemon, honey, and whiskey. In Kentucky, the iconic toddy is touted as a medicinal cure-all for any cough, sore throat, or fever. Kids are given a nonalcoholic version. Toddies beg for experimentation with the hot beverages used as the base and the sweeteners they're paired with. But keep in mind that heat raises the sensory perception of bourbon, so use less of a lower-proof whiskey to keep it from overwhelming the drink.

WHY THE FEMALE NOSE IS BETTER

Because of evolution, women have a genetic advantage that makes it easier for them to detect different scents. Women have 40 percent more cells in the human olfactory bulb than men. Studies have shown that females are unconsciously attracted to males whose scent indicates a different immune system from hers. When two people with different immune systems produce offspring, this advances human immunity to keep up with genetic changes that cause bacteria and parasites to become more infectious. What does this female advantage mean for bourbon? Women's innate ability to detect and identify scents puts them at an advantage when nosing whiskey, but experience and sensory training can improve any nose, male or female. The best sensory specialists are always training.

Tea Toddy.

Tea Toddy

One of my favorite variations on the toddy uses hot tea instead of hot water as the base. When making a medicinal toddy to soothe a sore throat and cough, I increase the amount of honey.

8 ounces boiling water (to warm the mug)

1½ ounces bourbon

½ ounce fresh lemon juice

1 tablespoon honey

4–6 ounces very hot tea (try peach or ginger tea)

Garnish: lemon wheel with cloves or cinnamon stick

Fill a mug with boiling water and let it sit for about 3 minutes while you gather the other ingredients. Empty the mug and discard the water. Add bourbon, lemon juice, honey, and tea to the mug. Stir with a spoon and check the taste. Add more lemon, honey, or bourbon if desired. Float a garnished lemon wheel on top.

High Tea Toddy variation: Build the toddy as described above, but use shortbread-infused bourbon (page 50) with a base of Earl Grey tea.

Cider Toddy

This cider-based toddy with a splash of maple syrup combines all the flavors of fall. Fresh pressed apple cider from a local orchard makes this toddy exceptional.

4–6 ounces apple cider

½ ounce maple syrup

½ ounce lemon juice

16 drops Old Forester's smoked cinnamon bitters (or 2 dashes of your favorite fall-flavored aromatic bitters)

1 dash ginger bitters

1½ ounces bourbon or whiskey

Garnish: apple slice, cinnamon stick

Fill a mug with hot water and set it aside. Combine apple cider, maple syrup, lemon juice, and bitters in a small saucepan and heat until steaming but not simmering (or heat in a microwave-safe container in the microwave). Add bourbon and stir to combine. Discard the water in the mug and pour the toddy into it. Garnish.

PROFESSIONAL TIP

Watch the whiskey's proof in warm cocktails. Anything over 100 proof, and the nose on the cocktail may become more of a burn!

Women love the complex flavors of bourbon and if a distillery makes great bourbon, women will buy it. In fact, Bourbon Women has had many blind tastings where women, without fail, choose the highest proof, most complex bourbons as their favorites."

–Susan Reigler,
Bourbon Women president,
2015–2017

Cider Toddy.

Rickhouse Hot Chocolate

Even in winter the rickhouses smell of whiskey and oak, and I wanted to combine those flavors in an easy-to-make bourbon hot chocolate. Topped with smoked whipped cream and a dusting of cinnamon, this drink is perfect for sipping in front of a fire.

10–12 ounces hot chocolate

2 ounces oaky bourbon (I used Woodford Reserve Double Oaked)

Dash ground cinnamon

Dash cayenne

1 bar spoon smoky Scotch whisky or mezcal

Garnish: 1–2 ounces smoked whipped cream (recipe to right), cinnamon, chocolate drizzle

Add ingredients to a warmed mug. Stir to combine. Garnish.

Smoked Whipped Cream

3 ounces whipping cream

½ ounce smoky Scotch whisky or mezcal

Combine ingredients in a small glass jar and shake until the cream thickens to an almost whipped consistency. Store any extra in the fridge. This is also a great topping in coffee or on cake.

Hot Buttered Bourbon

The addition of spices and brown sugar to this hot buttered rum variant makes an insanely vibrant drink. The five minutes it takes to make the hot buttered rum mix is well worth the effort for the aroma and flavors it provides.

6 ounces apple cider

2 tablespoons room-temperature hot buttered rum mix (recipe to right)

½ ounce Ballotin caramel turtle whiskey

1½ ounces low-proof bourbon

Whipped cream float (optional)

Garnish: cinnamon stick, star anise

Heat apple cider in a microwave-proof mug until very hot but not boiling. Add hot buttered rum mix, whiskey, and bourbon and stir well. Warm an additional 20–30 seconds in the microwave, if necessary. Top with whipped cream if desired and garnish.

Hot Buttered Rum Mix

1 stick butter (room temperature)

½ cup brown sugar

1½ teaspoons cinnamon

½ teaspoon ground nutmeg

½ teaspoon ground ginger

1½ teaspoons vanilla

Cream ingredients with a mixer or mix well by hand. Store in a small jar in the fridge.

Hot Buttered Bourbon.

10 | BOURBON DESSERT COCKTAILS

Sweets in a Glass

Bourbon Women Susan Reigler (center) and Peggy Noe Stevens (right) with Eric Gregory (left), head of the Kentucky Distillers Association. (Photo courtesy of Kentucky Distillers Association)

Diva's Envy

This prize-winning recipe by Beth Burrows, formerly of Down One Bourbon Bar in Louisville and now Jim Beam brand ambassador, makes a decadent chocolate dessert cocktail. I distinctly remember tasting it at the very first Bourbon Women SIPosium at French Lick Resort in Indiana, and everyone had one in hand.

---

2 ounces 86.6-proof bourbon

1 ounce Godiva dark chocolate liqueur

½ ounce cinnamon simple syrup

5 drops chocolate bitters

Garnish: cookie dough ball (egg free) and chocolate straw

Combine bourbon, liqueur, and simple syrup and shake with ice. Strain into a coupe glass. Top with chocolate bitters and garnish.

By Beth Burrows, 2014 Bourbon Women "Not Your Pink Drink" professional winner

There are many magnificent bourbon and dessert pairings. Adding just an ounce or two of bourbon to cakes, brownies, or whipped cream provides richness and complexity. So why not have a bourbon cocktail for dessert instead?

For bourbon enthusiasts hoping to convert their non-whiskey-drinking friends, getting them to fall in love with a bourbon dessert cocktail is the perfect strategy. These decadent cocktails belong in the home bartender's tool set because of the magic that happens when bourbon blends with chocolate, caramel, nuts, and cream.

Orange You Glad It's Bourbon?

This ginger-chocolate cocktail might have the old-fashioned as its base, but its flavors diverge wildly because the bourbon is infused with cacao nibs. My best advice is to let the popsicle garnish soak up the cocktail and save it as a boozy treat to eat at the end. (See cover photo.)

1¾ ounces chocolate-infused bourbon (recipe follows)

½ ounce Big O ginger liqueur

2 teaspoons vanilla simple syrup (see recipe on page 174)

3 dashes Scrappy's orange bitters

Garnish: chocolate pieces and 1 Trader Joe's tangerine cream popsicle or any orange cream popsicle

Combine ingredients in a mixing glass and add ice. Stir for 30 seconds. Strain into a chilled rocks glass filled with ice. Garnish.

Chocolate-Infused Bourbon

1½ cups bourbon (90–95 proof)

¼ cup cacao nibs

1 ounce simple syrup (optional)

Add bourbon and cacao nibs to a mason jar and seal. Infuse in a cool, dark place for at least 48 hours and up to 1 week. Each day, agitate the infusion and start checking the flavor after 48 hours. Once you love the flavor, strain the infusion through a metal sieve and store it in a clean glass jar. If you prefer a sweeter chocolate-infused whiskey, add simple syrup to the jar and store it in the fridge.

Bananas Foster Manhattan

As soon as I bought a bottle of Giffard banana liqueur, I knew I wanted to create a Bananas Foster–themed Manhattan. The salted caramel syrup imparts the caramel flavors of the flambéed bananas. This Manhattan is easy to make and even easier to sip.

2 ounces midproof bourbon

½ ounce salted caramel syrup (not cream based)

1 ounce Giffard Banane du Brèsil

12 drops Bittermens Elemakule Tiki bitters

2 dashes Fee Brothers black walnut bitters

Garnish: caramelized banana slices, mint leaves

Combine ingredients in a mixing glass. Add ice and stir until well chilled, about 30 seconds. Strain into a chilled cocktail glass. Caramelize banana slices with a kitchen torch and add as garnish, along with mint leaves.

Bourbon Affogato

Affogato is an Italian dessert that features hot espresso poured over vanilla or coffee gelato, but everything's better with bourbon. Make sure the coffee is hot and the ice cream is cold. Watching the two melt together can be mesmerizing. The recipe calls for vanilla gelato, but feel free to substitute your favorite flavor of gelato or ice cream (I like black raspberry).

1 scoop vanilla gelato

1 ounce hot espresso

1 ounce bourbon

Garnish: mint sprig

Combine hot espresso and bourbon right before serving. Pour over gelato in a chilled glass and garnish. Serve immediately.

Bananas Foster Manhattan.

Coffee-Cherry Smash.

Coffee-Cherry Smash

Although the combination of coffee and cherries is not as common as chocolate and cherries, it's a fantastic flavor pairing. The bitter, roasted, earthy notes from the coffee balance the sweet, fruity notes of the cherries. It's a magical combination to sip after dinner.

6 large pitted sweet cherries

½ ounce coffee simple syrup (see recipe on page 67)

½ ounce coffee liqueur

½ ounce cherry liqueur

2 ounces bourbon or rye whiskey

Garnish: cherries, mint sprig

"My favorite bourbon is Kentucky bourbon."

—Peggy Noe Stevens, founder, Bourbon Women

Place cherries and simple syrup in the bottom of a shaker. Muddle to release the cherries' juices. Add liqueurs and whiskey. Fill with ice and shake until very cold. Strain into a rocks glass filled with ice. Garnish.

Gettin' Lucky Tonight

Nutella + whiskey = heaven. Whether you make this cocktail for a get-together with friends or a romantic evening with your sweetheart, you'll love it. It's a decadent, sweet dessert in liquid form. Use the leftover chocolate sauce for whatever's on the menu for dessert.

1½ ounces 100-proof bourbon

1 ounce Nutella chocolate sauce (recipe follows)

½ ounce Ballotin chocolate whiskey

¼ ounce Rivulet artisan pecan liqueur

Garnish: Nutella, crushed roasted hazelnuts

Spread a bit of Nutella on the outside rim of a chilled martini glass and press hazelnuts into the Nutella. Set aside. Combine ingredients in a shaker and fill with ice. Shake for 10–12 seconds and double-strain into the prepared martini glass.

Nutella Chocolate Sauce

4 ounces bourbon cream

4 tablespoons Nutella

Warm bourbon cream slightly and add Nutella. Stir until well combined. This will solidify when refrigerated, but it can be reheated to return it to a liquid state.

Maple-Caramel Long John

This cocktail came together when I experimented with bourbon, bourbon cream, and caramel liqueur: it was mind-blowing. It inspired a series of five donut cocktails that I still make to this day. Be aware that this recipe is perfect for a bourbon newbie, but an experienced bourbon drinker probably needs a higher bourbon ratio and proof and less of the sweet elements.

1 ounce bourbon

1 ounce Buffalo Trace bourbon cream

1 ounce Stroopwafel caramel liqueur (or any caramel liqueur)

1 ounce cake vodka (optional; if you omit it, increase bourbon to 2 ounces)

½ ounce maple syrup liqueur (don't use maple syrup; it may cause curdling)

Garnish: cinnamon stick, donut hole with maple glaze (recipe follows)

Combine ingredients in a shaking tin. Fill with ice and shake for 10–12 seconds. Strain into a chilled rocks glass with one large-format ice cube. Garnish (excessively, if you like).

Maple Glaze

2 tablespoons butter

¼ cup maple syrup

½ cup powdered sugar

Heat butter and maple syrup until combined. Add powdered sugar. Whisk until perfectly smooth and allow to cool slightly. Use to glaze donut holes for garnish or to dip the entire rim of the glass. (Good luck not eating it by the spoonful.)

BOURBON AND FOOD PAIRINGS

Everyone loves a great food and whiskey pairing. I suggest you step outside the ordinary cheese or chocolate pairings and try bourbon with donuts, cookies, or brownies. Gather three or four whiskeys and three or four food items. Nose the bourbons for notes that tie in with the specific desserts. You could also do a pairing with a classic cocktail such as an old-fashioned, Manhattan, or Boulevardier. The key is to find matches that either complement each other or contrast and balance each other.

Maple-Caramel Long John.

Peach Smash

This traditional drink from my family vacations at Pawleys Island in South Carolina is usually made with rum, but the combination of peaches and bourbon is a match made in heaven. This recipe makes two drinks, but it can easily be scaled up for any number of bourbon lovers.

½ cup (4 ounces) low-proof bourbon

1 teaspoon vanilla extract

1 ounce ginger syrup (optional)

1 cup vanilla ice cream

1½–2 cups frozen peaches, slightly thawed

Garnish: peach slice, freshly grated nutmeg

Add bourbon, vanilla extract, ginger syrup (if using), ice cream, and frozen peaches to a blender in that order. Blend to a thick, creamy milkshake consistency. Pour into large wineglasses and garnish.

Kentucky Coquito

Based on a Puerto Rican version of eggless eggnog, this drink substitutes midproof bourbon for spiced rum. It's perfect for converting non-bourbon-drinking friends who like tropical drinks. This recipe makes about a liter of coquito.

1 (15-ounce) can Coco Lopez cream of coconut

1 (14-ounce) can sweetened condensed milk

1 (12-ounce) can evaporated milk

1½ cups midproof bourbon

3 ounces Amaretto (or substitute 1 teaspoon almond extract)

1 ounce St. Elizabeth allspice dram

½ teaspoon ground cinnamon

⅛ teaspoon ground cloves

¼ teaspoon ground nutmeg

1 teaspoon vanilla extract

Garnish: ground nutmeg or cinnamon stick

Combine ingredients in a blender and blend on high for 1–2 minutes until very well combined. Pour into empty bourbon bottles or jars and refrigerate overnight. Serve very cold, shaking vigorously before pouring into serving glasses. Garnish.

Kentucky Coquito.

Pecan Sticky Bun.

Pecan Sticky Bun

This cocktail is nothing but decadence. The flavors are most often associated with a breakfast sticky bun, but they make a delicious dessert cocktail for those who love the combination of bourbon and pecan.

2 ounces bourbon (I used Old Bardstown bottled in bond)

½ ounce Monin's cinnamon roll syrup (or vanilla-cinnamon simple syrup)

½ ounce Rivulet pecan liqueur

½ ounce caramel liqueur (noncreamy; I used Stroopwafel caramel)

3 dashes Fee Brothers black walnut bitters

Garnish: donut holes frosted with cream cheese icing (recipe follows), candied pecans, or ½ sticky bun

Combine ingredients in a mixing glass. Add ice and stir until well combined, about 30 seconds. Strain into a coupe glass and add garnish. Prepare for the sugar rush.

Cream Cheese Icing

2 ounces cream cheese, softened

2 tablespoons unsalted butter, softened

1 teaspoon bourbon

Pinch salt

½ cup powdered sugar

1 ounce milk or cream (as needed)

Mix cream cheese and butter until smooth. Add bourbon and salt. Slowly add powdered sugar, beating well until smooth. Add enough milk or cream to achieve the desired consistency.

Cherry SIP-Shake

Created to celebrate a virtual SIPosium in the summer of 2020, this recipe makes two boozy cherry milkshakes.

4 ounces 100-proof bourbon

¾ ounce lemon simple syrup (see recipe on page 75) *or* ½ ounce simple syrup and juice from 1 lemon wedge

1 cup vanilla ice cream

2 cups frozen sweet cherries, pitted

Garnish: mint sprig, cherries

Put ingredients in a blender in the order listed above. Blend on high until smooth. Pour into two fancy glasses and add garnish.

HOW TO AVOID CURDLED COCKTAILS

Milk and cream products curdle in the presence of acid such as citrus, sodas, or liqueurs with a high acid content. Curdled cocktails look terrible and feel gritty in the mouth. To avoid curdling, here are three tips: (1) Use heavy cream; don't substitute milk or low-fat products. The fat keeps the cream from curdling. (2) Add cream to the cocktail shaker last and shake immediately. The fast dilution prevents curdling. (3) Avoid adding cream or creamy liqueurs to cocktails with citrus or other acidic ingredients.

Cherry SIP-Shake.

Apple Fritter.

Apple Fritter

This cocktail tastes like a smooth bite of a boozy apple fritter. The secret ingredient is apple cider molasses. Its sweet, tart, concentrated apple flavor is magical in cocktails and other beverages, in desserts, and on hot biscuits. It's available online, but during apple season, it's easy to make at home.

1 ounce Wilderness Trail rye whiskey or high-rye bourbon

1 ounce Copper & Kings Floodwall aged apple brandy

½ ounce apple cider molasses (see recipe on page 69)

¼ ounce Trader Vic's macadamia nut liqueur

¼ ounce Monin's cinnamon bun syrup (or vanilla-cinnamon simple syrup)

2 dashes Bar Keep organic apple bitters

1 dash Hella Bitters ginger bitters

Garnish: cinnamon sugar (optional); apple fan, apple fritter slice, cinnamon stick

If desired, dip the rim of a rocks glass in cinnamon sugar and set aside. Combine ingredients in a mixing glass. Add ice and stir until well chilled, about 30 seconds. Strain into a rocks glass with ice and add garnish.

11 | PARTY COCKTAILS

Batching Bourbon Drinks Like a Pro

Copper Mule Bourbon Slush

Nothing makes a drink more local than using a local bourbon, and every bourbon book needs a great bourbon slush recipe for summer soirees and easy entertaining. This one makes 1 gallon, and the best thing about a bourbon slush is that leftovers can go back into the freezer for the next backyard party.

2 (12-ounce) cans frozen lemonade concentrate

½ (12-ounce) can frozen orange juice concentrate

4 (12-ounce) cans water

1½ (12-ounce) cans Copper Mule bourbon

1 batch sweet tea syrup (recipe follows)

Thaw juices and pour them into a gallon-sized or larger container. Add water, bourbon, and sweet tea syrup and stir. Place the container in the freezer and stir every few hours until set, about 8 hours or overnight.

To serve, rake slush with a fork and scoop into serving glasses. Serve with a spoon or straw.

Sweet Tea Syrup

1 tea bag

2 cups water

1 cup sugar

Steep tea bag in boiling water. Squeeze water out of tea bag, remove, and add sugar. Stir until sugar is dissolved.

Missouri branch of Bourbon Women—submitted by Jeanne Gosen, Copper Mule Distillery

As a host, you want to visit with your guests, not spend all evening making cocktails. The easiest solution is to batch cocktails ahead of time. I make batches of several different old-fashioneds and Manhattans for parties and present them in old bourbon bottles. Guests can pour their own cocktails and try a little of everything if they like.

Batching cocktails isn't difficult, but it involves more than simply multiplying ingredients. It's easier to balance flavors and avoid bitterness if you batch spirit-forward cocktails rather than lighter, juice-filled cocktails. The flavor of fresh juice degrades rather quickly, meaning that you have to squeeze citrus fruits on the day of the party. And for optimum taste, all batched cocktails with fruit juice should be consumed that day too.

How to Batch a Spirit-Forward Cocktail

Bourbon enthusiasts love a great cocktail, but we want to be able to taste the bourbon. Many prefer spirit-forward cocktails, meaning that the main ingredients are spirits, not mixers or juices. For example, old-fashioneds, Manhattans, Boulevardiers, and Sazeracs don't contain any fresh juice, cream, or mixers, so they're easy to batch in advance and still maintain the flavor of a freshly mixed cocktail.

Bitters can be an especially tricky ingredient in batched cocktails. Simply multiplying the ingredients and using the full amount of bitters may result in a cocktail that is overly bitter and harsh. And the longer the cocktail sits in a batch, the more bitter it becomes. To avoid this problem, reduce the amount of bitters by one-half or one-third and do a taste test. Compare the flavor of the batch to a single serving of the cocktail and tweak the amount of bitters, adding more as needed.

I use the following process—basically, converting ounces to cups—to create a batch of eight to ten cocktails, which usually fits in an empty 750-milliliter bottle:

1. For each element in the cocktail, excluding bitters and garnish, convert ounces to cups. For example, if an old-fashioned calls for 2 ounces of bourbon, use 2 cups. Similarly, convert ½ ounce of simple syrup to ½ cup.

2. Add the ingredients to a pitcher or a 4- to 6-cup container.

3. Add ½ to ⅔ of the total amount of bitters to the pitcher.

4. Stir.

5. Add water: If the batch is less than 2½ cups, use ½ cup water. If the batch is more than 3½ cups, add ½ to 1 cup water. If the batch is between these two volumes, start with ½ cup water, taste, and adjust as needed.

6. Stir again and do a taste test.

7. Adjust bitters or water as needed. The proof of the cocktail will taste hot because the alcohol is not chilled, but it shouldn't burn the roof of your mouth.

8. Label, date, and fully chill before serving.

To create larger batches, I multiply the ingredients in ounces by the expected number of servings (except for the bitters, of course) and then convert to cups. I *always* reduce the amount of bitters by one-half to one-third to keep them from becoming too aggressive.

MAKING USE OF THE BOURBON YOU HATE

If you have a bottle of bourbon that you can't stand, the best solution is to find someone who loves that particular bottle and make her a batched cocktail using that bourbon. She won't ever know you sampled from the bottle, and she'll be thrilled to have a bottle of ready-to-drink cocktails.

Batched Brown Derby cocktails at the 2019 SIPosium. (Photo by Chris Joyce KY)

Dos and Don'ts for Batching Cocktails

Do a taste test as you batch and again before you serve. Check the cocktail's balance after the batch is mixed, and do another taste test before serving. If the cocktail is too sweet, the addition of bitters can balance the flavors.

Do add water if you're serving straight from the batched bottle. If guests or servers will be pouring straight from the bottles containing the batched cocktails, add water—about ½ to ¾ cup per 750-milliliter batch.

Don't add the full amount of bitters at first. Reduce the total amount by one-half or one-third and do a taste test. Bitters can always be added, but it's impossible to fix the cocktail once you've added too much.

Don't stress about chilling the glasses at a large party. If you have the space and a means to chill the glasses, do so. But if you're working with plastic cups or limited space, provide smaller servings so the cocktail won't get too warm as the guests drink it.

> ## HOW TO BATCH A HIGHBALL, MULE, OR BUBBLY COCKTAIL
>
> Combine all the ingredients except the carbonated beverage or sparkling wine in the quantities needed (making sure to reduce the amount of bitters). Chill in the fridge. To serve, put the premixed ingredients in a glass, add ice, and top with well-chilled soda or sparkling wine.

Do simplify the garnish. For example, rather than creating 30 citrus peel roses, use a simple citrus twist or dried orange. Fresh fruit skewers can be prepared in advance. Even simpler is a flower, a single herb leaf, a dried spice, or a candy garnish that can be added quickly.

Do provide a sample cocktail, on display and garnished, for guests to see if they're pouring their own. When guests are pouring their own cocktails, they will be able to see which garnish goes with the drink and how to place it.

Don't make the drink too far in advance. Batching cocktails a day or two in advance is fine, but not a month before the party (unless you're bottle-aging cocktails on purpose, of course).

> ## MIXING IN FRONT OF A CROWD
>
> If you prefer to show your guests the magic of stirring or shaking a cocktail, omit the water from the batching process. At showtime, pour 2½–3 ounces of the cocktail mix into a mixing glass or shaker filled with ice. Stir or shake as you would for a single cocktail, about 30 seconds, and strain into a prepared glass.

Batched Fleur-de-Lis Manhattan

This batched Manhattan can be stored in the fridge in an empty 750-milliliter bottle. Chilling is mandatory, as it is served without ice. For larger pours or parties, you can double or triple the recipe (this one makes 8–10 cocktails). For the single-serving recipe, see chapter 5.

1½ cups 100-proof bourbon

¾ cup Ballotin Bourbon Ball whiskey

¾ cup Chambord black raspberry liqueur

8–12 drops Scrappy's cardamom bitters

8–12 dashes chocolate bitters

½–¾ cup water

Garnish: bourbon ball, fresh raspberry, grated chocolate

Combine ingredients in a large pitcher and stir well. Taste the cocktail for balance, and if it is too sweet or the balance is off, add more bitters judiciously. Transfer to an empty 750-milliliter bottle, seal, and chill for several hours or overnight in the fridge.

Before serving, chill for 30 minutes in the freezer (don't leave the bottle in the freezer overnight, as it may freeze completely). If guests will be pouring their own cocktails, place the bottle in an ice bucket to keep it cold. Serve in a coupe or martini glass and add garnish.

EDIBLE FLOWERS

Flowers look gorgeous on cocktails, but you have to do your homework to keep your guests safe. Make sure the flower isn't poisonous, and check that it's organic and safe for human consumption. Many flowers sold in flower shops have been sprayed with insecticides or toxic chemicals to preserve them. Search for edible flowers online to meet your garnish needs.

Batched Classic Manhattan

You can easily mix up a batch of Manhattans before a group comes over. This recipe makes 8–10 cocktails.

2 cups midproof bourbon

1 cup Carpano Antica Formula sweet vermouth

6–10 dashes cherry bitters

6–10 dashes orange bitters

½–¾ cup water

Garnish: cocktail cherry

Combine ingredients in a large pitcher and stir well. Taste the cocktail for balance, and if it is too sweet or the balance is off, add more bitters judiciously. Transfer to an empty bottle, seal, and chill for several hours or overnight in the fridge.

Before serving, chill for 30 minutes in the freezer (don't leave the bottle in the freezer overnight, as it may freeze completely). If guests will be pouring their own cocktails, place the bottle in an ice bucket to keep it cold. Serve in a coupe or martini glass and add garnish.

Batched Cocoa Manhattan

This easily batched cocktail turns a classic Manhattan into a decadent chocolate treat that still celebrates the bourbon. This recipe makes 8–10 cocktails. For the single-serving version, see chapter 5.

2 cups low- to midproof bourbon

¾ cup Ballotin chocolate whiskey or other non-cream-based chocolate liqueur

½ cup Meletti or Averna amaro

12–20 dashes chocolate bitters

12–20 dashes cherry bitters

½–¾ cup water

Garnish: grated chocolate or chocolate square

Combine ingredients in a large pitcher and stir well. Taste the cocktail for balance, and if it is too sweet or the balance is off, add more bitters judiciously. Transfer to an empty bottle, seal, and chill for several hours or overnight in the fridge.

Before serving, chill for 30 minutes in the freezer (don't leave the bottle in the freezer overnight, as it may freeze completely). If guests will be pouring their own cocktails, place the bottle in an ice bucket to keep it cold. Serve in a coupe or martini glass and add garnish.

Batched Manhattans with different garnishes.

Batched Midnight Hour

This batched cocktail re-creates the flavors of the first Black Manhattan I ever had. I fell in love with amaro that night, and the Black Manhattan is still my favorite of all the classic variations (see the photo on page 91). This recipe makes 8–10 cocktails.

"The best etiquette you can have is to make your guests feel comfortable in your own home. I want people to know we have a gracious lifestyle in bourbon and we have a heart for hospitality in bourbon, and when you put those two things together you are going to enjoy your guests and your guests are going to enjoy you."

—Peggy Noe Stevens, founder, Bourbon Women

2 cups bourbon (I use Johnny Drum bourbon)

¼ cup Carpano Antica sweet vermouth

¾ cup Averna amaro

32–40 drops Woodford's sorghum and sassafras bitters

16–24 drops Bittermens Elekamule Tiki bitters

½–¾ cup water

Garnish: lemon peel, cocktail cherry

Combine ingredients in a large pitcher and stir until well combined. Taste the cocktail for balance, and if it is too sweet or the balance is off, add more bitters judiciously. Transfer to an empty bottle, seal, and chill for several hours or overnight in the fridge.

Before serving, chill for 30 minutes in the freezer (don't leave the bottle in the freezer overnight, as it may freeze completely). If guests will be pouring their own cocktails, place the bottle in an ice bucket to keep it cold. Serve in a coupe or martini glass and add garnish.

Batched Classic Old-Fashioned

Bourbon lovers and the bourbon curious can sip on an old-fashioned all night long. This easy brown sugar old-fashioned batches beautifully for an event or can be kept in the fridge for evenings when you don't feel like making a cocktail from scratch. This recipe makes 8–10 cocktails.

2 cups bourbon

½ cup brown sugar simple syrup

½ cup water

8–12 dashes orange bitters

8–12 dashes aromatic or cherry bitters

Garnish: cocktail cherry, orange peel

Combine ingredients in a large pitcher. Taste the cocktail for balance, and if it is too sweet or the balance is off, add more bitters judiciously. Transfer to an empty bottle, seal, and chill for several hours or overnight in the fridge.

Before serving, chill for 30 minutes in the freezer (don't leave the bottle in the freezer overnight, as it may freeze completely). If guests will be pouring their own cocktails, place the bottle in an ice bucket to keep it cold. Serve in a rocks glass over ice and add garnish.

Batched Kentucky Smolder

This bold old-fashioned (see chapter 4 for the single-serving version) uses a high-proof bourbon and some smoked elements to keep bourbon enthusiasts interested and happy. This recipe makes 8–10 cocktails.

2 cups Old Forester Whiskey Row 1920 or Pikesville rye

½ cup demerara simple syrup

16–30 dashes Hella Bitters smoked chili bitters

½ cup water

Garnish: charred cinnamon sticks

Combine ingredients in a large container. Taste the cocktail for balance, and if it is too sweet or the balance is off, add more bitters judiciously. Transfer to an empty bottle, seal, and chill for several hours or overnight in the fridge.

Before serving, chill for 30 minutes in the freezer (don't leave the bottle in the freezer overnight, as it may freeze completely). If guests will be pouring their own cocktails, place the bottle in an ice bucket to keep it cold. Serve in a rocks glass over ice and add garnish.

Batched Toasted S'mores Old-Fashioned

The only hard part about making this batched old-fashioned is not eating the toasted marshmallows before you serve them to guests. You can make tiny s'mores to garnish each cocktail, but it's easier to torch marshmallows on a cocktail pick and add them to each drink (see the photo on page 30). This recipe makes 8–10 cocktails.

1¾ cups bourbon

¼ cup crème de cacao or chocolate whiskey

½ cup toasted marshmallow simple syrup (see recipe on page 66)

60–100 drops (½–1 teaspoon) Bittermens Xocolatl mole chocolate bitters

2½ tablespoons peated whiskey or smoky mezcal

½–¾ cup water

Garnish: tiny s'mores or torched marshmallows

Combine ingredients in an empty bourbon bottle and agitate. Taste the cocktail for balance, and if it is too sweet or the balance is off, add more bitters judiciously. Seal the bottle and chill for several hours or overnight in the fridge.

Before serving, chill for 30 minutes in the freezer (don't leave the bottle in the freezer overnight, as it may freeze completely). If guests will be pouring their own cocktails, place the bottle in an ice bucket to keep it cold. Serve in a rocks glass over ice and add garnish.

"I give bottles of bourbon and my bourbon books as gifts. Often together."

—Susan Reigler, Bourbon Women president, 2015–2017

Batched Banana Bread Old-Fashioned

Another hit with bourbon drinkers, this batched old-fashioned celebrates a whiskey classic with the banana flavors found in many bourbons (see the photo on page 65). This recipe makes 8–10 cocktails.

2 cups bourbon (Old Forester Signature 100-proof preferred)

½ cup banana simple syrup (see recipe on page 64)

10–14 dashes Fee Brothers black walnut bitters

½–¾ cup water

Garnish: orange peel and vanilla bean or cinnamon stick

Combine ingredients in an empty whiskey bottle and agitate. Taste the cocktail for balance, and if it is too sweet or the balance is off, add more bitters judiciously. Seal the bottle and chill for several hours or overnight in the fridge.

Before serving, chill for 30 minutes in the freezer (don't leave the bottle in the freezer overnight, as it may freeze completely). If guests will be pouring their own cocktails, place the bottle in an ice bucket to keep it cold. Serve in a rocks glass over ice and add garnish.

Batched Prince Harry Old-Fashioned

The honey and ginger flavors in this sweet old-fashioned make it a great batched cocktail for fall and winter gatherings, and the simple candied ginger garnish looks beautiful. This recipe makes 8–10 cocktails.

1½ cups Elijah Craig small-batch bourbon

½ cup Domaine de Canton ginger liqueur

½ cup honey syrup

12–20 dashes Hella Bitters ginger bitters

½–¾ cup water

Garnish: slice of candied ginger

PARTY TIP

I often make cocktails instead of food to bring to potlucks or give as hostess gifts. No one seems to mind that I don't bring a cheese ball or a plate of cookies if I show up with ready-to-drink cocktails, ice, and cups. I usually make two batches of cocktails: one for the crowd, and one for the hosts to enjoy after the party.

Combine ingredients in an empty whiskey bottle and agitate. Taste the cocktail for balance, and if it is too sweet or the balance is off, add more bitters judiciously. Seal the bottle and chill for several hours or overnight in the fridge.

Before serving, chill for 30 minutes in the freezer (don't leave the bottle in the freezer overnight, as it may freeze completely). If guests will be pouring their own cocktails, place the bottle in an ice bucket to keep it cold. Serve in a rocks glass over ice and add garnish.

Tailgate Sour

At a Bourbon Women event held at the governor's mansion, we were served a very fancy, flower-garnished sour. When I went to the bar and asked for the recipe, the bar manager laughed and gave me the following. I call it a Tailgate Sour because it's easy to make and easy to batch, and when it's served to a group of friends, you don't need anything else. This recipe makes 12 cocktails.

1 12-ounce can organic lemonade concentrate

1¼ cans bourbon

1½ cans water

½ can fresh orange juice

20–32 dashes black walnut, orange, or lavender bitters (optional)

Garnish: lemon or orange wheel, fresh lavender or mint sprig (if available)

Combine ingredients in a large pitcher, starting with the lower amount of bitters. Stir and taste. Add more bitters if necessary. Transfer to a bottle and chill for several hours or overnight in the fridge. If guests will be pouring their own cocktails, place the bottle in an ice bucket to keep it cold. Serve over ice and add garnish.

Batched Classic Mint Julep

If you don't have enough metal julep cups, these cocktails can be served in short glasses filled with crushed or pellet ice (not cubes). Use plenty of fresh mint sprigs, and serve each drink with a straw. This recipe makes 8–10 cocktails. If there are any leftovers, remove the mint sprigs and store the remainder in the fridge. Leaving the mint in the batch will turn it bitter.

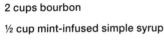

2 cups bourbon

½ cup mint-infused simple syrup

½ cup water

2–3 fresh mint sprigs

Garnish: fresh mint sprigs

Add bourbon, syrup, and water to an empty whiskey bottle and agitate. Seal the bottle and chill for several hours or overnight in the fridge. About 20 minutes before serving, add spanked mint sprigs to the bottle or transfer to a pitcher. Serve over crushed ice in julep cups and add garnish and a straw.

> **PARTY TIP**
>
> If you're struggling to find a beautiful garnish, dehydrated citrus chips look great when paired with a fresh herb sprig. Fresh citrus garnishes can be prepared earlier in the day but must be wrapped in damp paper towels and refrigerated so they don't dry out. Frozen berries look striking in cocktails served in wineglasses over ice, and they help keep the drink cold.

Chocolate-Mint Julep.

Batched Chocolate-Mint Julep

Although juleps are typically associated with the summer months, this batched version works as a tasty December cocktail for the holidays. Add a single chocolate mint cookie to the cocktail right next to the mint sprig for garnish. This recipe makes 8–10 cocktails. If there are any leftovers, remove the mint sprigs and store the remainder in the fridge. Leaving the mint in the batch will turn it bitter.

1½ cups low- to midproof bourbon

1½ cups Ballotin chocolate mint whiskey

8–10 dashes Scrappy's chocolate bitters

½ cup water

2–3 fresh mint sprigs

Garnish: fresh mint sprigs and chocolate mint cookie

Add bourbon, whiskey, bitters, and water to an empty whiskey bottle and agitate. Chill for several hours or overnight in the fridge. About 20 minutes before serving, add mint sprigs to the bottle. Serve in julep cups with crushed ice and add garnish and a straw.

Batched Peach, Please Julep

This batched version of the julep in chapter 8 relies on simple aromatics to add basil flavor to the cocktail. Although you can infuse peach simple syrup with basil, that method works best with cooked peach syrup, and I prefer the taste of fresh, uncooked peaches here. This recipe makes 8–10 cocktails. If there are any leftovers, remove the basil sprigs and store the remainder in the fridge. Leaving the basil in the batch will turn it bitter.

2 cups low- or midproof bourbon

½ cup peach simple syrup (see recipe on page 168)

½ cup Giffard Pêche de Vigne peach liqueur

½ cup water

2–3 basil sprigs

Fresh peach slices

Garnish: fresh basil sprigs, fresh peach slices

Add bourbon, syrup, peach liqueur, and water to an empty whiskey bottle and agitate. Chill for several hours or overnight in the fridge. About 20 minutes before serving, add basil sprigs and fresh peach slices to the bottle. Serve over crushed ice in julep cups and add garnish and a straw.

Batched Ginger-Chai Julep

Dress up a fall party with ginger-chai juleps—a simple combination to celebrate the fall meet at the horse track or all things autumn (see the photo on page 171). This recipe makes 8–10 cocktails. If there are any leftovers, remove the mint and cinnamon and store the remainder in the fridge. Leaving them in the batch will turn it bitter.

1½ cups midproof bourbon

½ cup ginger liqueur

½ cup chai simple syrup (see recipe on page 170)

½ cup water

2–3 fresh mint sprigs

Cinnamon sticks

Garnish: mint sprigs, candied ginger, cinnamon stick

Add bourbon, ginger liqueur, chai syrup, and water to an empty whiskey bottle and agitate. Chill for several hours or overnight in the fridge. About 20 minutes before serving, add mint sprigs and cinnamon sticks to the bottle. Serve over crushed ice in julep cups and add garnish and a straw.

12 | BOURBON WOMEN'S "NOT YOUR PINK DRINK" CONTEST WINNERS

Samantha Montgomery
Bardstown Bourbon Company
2018 Not Your Pink Drink
Cocktail Recipe Winner
Professional Division

BW
BOURBON · WOMEN
"Kickin' Dicksie"

The author awards Samantha Montgomery the 2018 "Not Your Pink Drink" professional award for her cocktail Kickin' Dicksie. (Photo by Chris Joyce KY)

Each year, Bourbon Women holds a competition for the best bourbon cocktail called the "Not Your Pink Drink" contest. The one rule? The cocktail cannot be pink, as members wanted to move away from "girly" cocktails. The winners are selected by a panel of Bourbon Women members, some of whom are on the board of directors. The judges evaluate the flavor, balance, creativity, presentation, and approachability of each cocktail. Over time, the contest has evolved from a gathering of the board of directors making and tasting the cocktails to an in-person contest where the finalists prepare their own drinks for the judges. There are amateur and professional categories, and the winning cocktails are presented at the annual Bourbon Women SIPosium, held in the late summer or early fall.

The "Not Your Pink Drink" contest started my bourbon cocktail obsession and led me to write this book. And although I occasionally make whiskey drinks that turn out a little bit pink, I still prefer the beauty of an amber-colored cocktail with the light shining through it. Every year, the judges are blown away by the creativity and passion of the participants, whose award-winning cocktails celebrate the flavors and aromas we all love in whiskeys. So mix up a few of these recipes and celebrate all things bourbon.

Life Is Peachy

By Tara VanderMolen, 2016 "Not Your Pink Drink" professional winner

This summertime old-fashioned with peach, basil, and cardamom will make a bourbon believer out of anyone. It was created by Tara VanderMolen, bartender and manager at the Osteria Rossa Restaurant.

2 ounces Maker's Mark bourbon

½ ounce lemon juice

½ ounce simple syrup

3 dashes cardamom bitters

2 large basil leaves, muddled

2 ounces fresh peaches, muddled

Garnish: fresh peach slice, basil sprig

Shake well with ice. Strain into an ice-filled rocks glass and add garnish.

Not Your Subourban Housewife

By Rachel Isaacs, 2012 "Not Your Pink Drink" professional winner

This easy, equal-parts cocktail combines bourbon, butterscotch, and hazelnut flavors with just a rinse of Grand Marnier for its citrus notes.

1 ounce 90-proof bourbon

1 ounce butterscotch schnapps

1 ounce Frangelico hazelnut liqueur

Splash Grand Marnier

Garnish: orange twist, dried apricot

Shake with ice and strain into a chilled martini glass rimmed with raw sugar. Garnish.

High Doll

By Karen Rego, 2012 "Not Your Pink Drink" amateur winner

This highball-esque cocktail is a delectable combination of bourbon, lime, Amaretto, and sparkling water.

1¼ ounces 90-proof bourbon

¾ ounce Amaretto

2 ounces chilled lime sparkling water

1 lime wedge

Garnish: orange slice

Pour bourbon and Amaretto into a glass filled with ice. Add sparkling water. Squeeze juice from the lime wedge into the glass and add the wedge. Stir gently. Garnish.

Palm Breeze

By Marla Zimmerman, 2013 "Not Your Pink Drink" amateur winner

Marla Zimmerman's citrus cooler features Four Roses Single Barrel bourbon and mixes the flavors of multiple citrus fruits in a highball-type cocktail that's perfect for warm weather.

1½ ounces Four Roses Single Barrel bourbon

2 dashes Peychaud's bitters

1 Splenda packet (¼ teaspoon)

1 slice orange

½ slice grapefruit

1 slice lemon

4 ounces club soda

¾ cup ice

Add bourbon, bitters, and Splenda to a tall glass and stir until Splenda dissolves. Add fruit slices, slightly squeezing each one to add juice to the mixture. Add club soda and then ice. Use one of the fruit slices on the rim of the glass as garnish.

BOURBON WOMEN SIPOSIUM

The annual meeting of Bourbon Women feels more like a reunion than a conference. You can't walk across the room without seeing a friend from an earlier event or a virtual tasting or a follower on social media. Powerful women in the bourbon and beverage industries meet each fall to bring consumers and producers together. From distillery and cooperage excursions to intimate dinners in storied members' homes, it's an event that's a year in the making. Each day starts with a toast and a tasting at about 9:00 a.m. (that's just how we roll). Head to **www.bourbonwomen.org** for the latest.

(Facing page) **Members of Bourbon Women on their way to the opening-night dinner at the 2018 SIPosium. (Photo by Chris Joyce KY)**

Kentucky Moon

By Alice Zoeller, 2014 "Not Your Pink Drink" amateur winner

This award-winner is a simple and timeless combination of bourbon, Grand Marnier, and Frangelico that can be thrown together at a moment's notice.

Grand Marnier (to coat the glass)

¼ ounce Frangelico

1 ounce 100-proof bourbon (Zoeller used Johnny Drum Private Stock)

Garnish: orange zest twist

Coat the inside of a chilled rocks glass with Grand Marnier and discard the excess. Add bourbon and Frangelico to the glass. Garnish.

Minted Gold

By Bob Knott, 2015 "Not Your Pink Drink" professional winner

Bob Knott of the Seelbach Hotel bar created this cocktail with layers of flavors from bourbon, citrus, honey, and ginger beer.

1½ ounces 80-proof bourbon

2 ounces fresh lemon juice

1 ounce honey syrup

Ginger beer

2 ounces fresh orange juice

Garnish: mint sprig

Add bourbon, honey syrup, and fruit juices to a shaker with ice. Shake and strain into a rocks glass. Top with ginger beer and garnish with a mint sprig.

French Quarter Manhattan

By Heather Wibbels, 2015 "Not Your Pink Drink" amateur winner

I won my first cocktail contest in 2015 with this recipe that combines the flavors of bourbon, pecan, and chocolate, served neat in a chilled martini glass. This was one of my early successes in getting my not-so-bourbon-centric husband to enjoy a bourbon cocktail.

2 ounces small-batch 90-proof bourbon

1 ounce Rivulet pecan liqueur

4–5 dashes chocolate bitters

Garnish: pralines or candied pecans

Add ingredients to a mixing glass filled with ice. Stir to combine. Strain into a chilled martini glass and garnish.

The Black Forest

By Heather Wibbels, 2016 "Not Your Pink Drink" amateur winner

This is my take on a chocolate and cherry bakery favorite that melds those two flavors with bourbon. If you can find a chocolate-covered cherry for the garnish, you won't regret the pairing.

1½ ounces 85- to 90-proof bourbon

¾ ounce chocolate whiskey or chocolate moonshine (60 proof)

½ ounce cherry liqueur

3 dashes chocolate bitters

1 dash cherry bitters

Garnish: Maraschino cherry, chocolate syrup (optional)

Place ingredients in a mixing glass and fill with ice. Stir. Strain into a chilled martini glass with a bit of chocolate syrup on the rim, if desired. Garnish with a cherry.

Blood Orange Manhattan

By Heather Wibbels, 2017 "Not Your Pink Drink" amateur winner

This cocktail calls for blood orange liqueur and a combination of cherry and orange bitters to create a citrusy, winter twist on a Manhattan.

2 ounces Old Forester 1870 bourbon

½ ounce sweet vermouth

¾ ounce blood orange liqueur

1 dash cherry bitters

2 dashes orange bitters

Garnish: blood orange wheel (in season) or orange peel twist

Combine ingredients in a mixing glass and fill with ice. Stir until well chilled, about 30 seconds. Strain into a chilled coupe or martini glass. Express the orange peel over the drink and rub the rim with it for an extra orange kick.

Kickin' Dicksie

By Samantha Montgomery, 2018 "Not Your Pink Drink" professional winner

The judges loved the way this cocktail evolved as it diluted slightly. Different layers of flavor bloomed at different points while tasting it, making it a delight from first sip to last.

¼ ounce Dixie black pepper vodka (80 proof)

½ ounce Meletti amaro (64 proof)

½ ounce Cardamaro (34 proof)

1½ ounces Fighting Cock bourbon (103 proof)

Garnish: ground black pepper, grapefruit twist

Stir ingredients in a mixing glass. Strain into a rocks glass over ice. Garnish.

Kombucha Bourbon Crush

By Dani Barrow, 2019 "Not Your Pink Drink" amateur winner

The earthy citrus of Dani Barrow's homemade kombucha elixir gets a little extra kick from ginger liqueur and a little extra sweetness from maple syrup. (Kombucha, a fermented, sweetened tea, often has juice, fruit, or other fruit flavorings added to it.)

1½ ounces Knob Creek small-batch bourbon

3 ounces homemade lemon-rosemary kombucha

½ ounce local maple syrup (plus extra to rim the glass)

¼ ounce ginger liqueur

Round ice cube

Garnish: pink Himalayan salt (rim), rosemary sprig

Rim half of a Collins glass with maple syrup and pink salt (the salty-sweet combination cuts the natural acidity of the lemon-based kombucha). Add remaining ingredients to the glass and gently stir to combine. Add ice cube and garnish with rosemary.

Kombucha Bourbon Crush. (Photo by Tracy Green/ Estes Public Relations)

Bourbon Pèche Highball

By Kendrick Pennington, 2021 "Not Your Pink Drink" amateur winner

This refreshing summery highball uses an unusual carbonated beverage to top the bourbon base. The fresh basil garnish and baking spice notes of the sugared rim balance the sourness and lovely peach flavor of the beer.

2 ounces Rabbit Hole Heigold bourbon

½ ounce Frangelico

2 dashes Old Forester smoked cinnamon bitters

1 dash black walnut bitters

Lineman's Pèche Lambic beer (peach)

Garnish: basil and dehydrated peach slices dusted with nutmeg, cinnamon, and brown sugar (recipe follows)

Dip the rim of a highball glass in water and then dip the rim in a dish containing a mixture of nutmeg, cinnamon, and brown sugar (as prepared for the dehydrated peaches below). Fill the glass with ice and set aside. In a mixing glass with ice, combine bourbon, Frangelico, and bitters. Stir for 15–30 seconds. Strain into the prepared highball glass. Top with Pèche Lambic beer. Garnish with dehydrated peach slices and basil.

Dehydrated Peaches

Slice peaches ½ inch thick and place on a rack on top of a baking sheet. Place the baking sheet in the oven on the lowest temperature and let the peaches dehydrate for a few hours. With a zester or grater, grate equal amounts of nutmeg and cinnamon into a dish and add an equal amount of brown sugar. Toss the dehydrated peaches in the sugar and spice mixture.

Pineapple Tattoo

By Molly Hollar, 2021 "Not Your Pink Drink" professional winner

A touch of umami from the miso syrup and roasted flavors from the pineapple turn this whiskey sour riff into a cocktail experience that highlights Rabbit Hole's spicy rye and builds complex layers of flavors with the bitters.

1½ ounces Rabbit Hole rye

1½ ounces roasted pineapple juice

¼ ounce lime juice

½ ounce miso syrup (recipe follows)

1 drop Chinese five-spice bitters

Garnish: orange zest

Add rye, juices, and miso syrup to a shaking tin and fill with ice. Shake for 10–12 seconds. Strain into a chilled Nick and Nora glass. Drop bitters on top and garnish.

Miso Syrup

1 cup dark brown sugar

1 cup water

2 heaping tablespoons white miso paste

In a small saucepan, bring ingredients to a boil. Then simmer on low heat for 1 minute, whisking frequently. Cool. Strain through a fine mesh strainer and store in the fridge for 3–4 weeks.

Judging at the 2019 "Not Your Pink Drink" competition. (Photo by Tracy Green/Estes Public Relations)

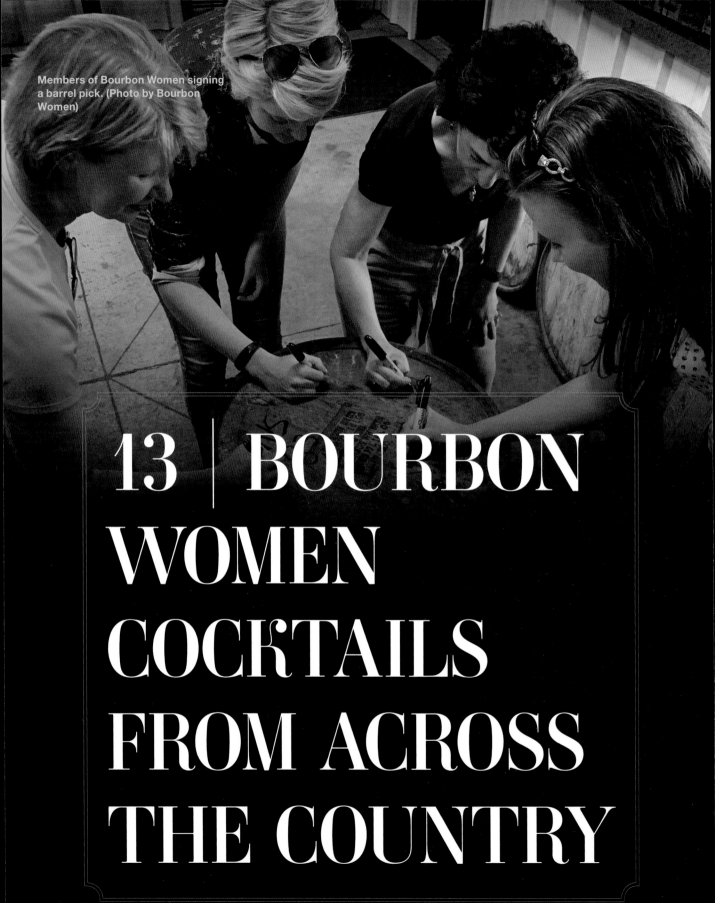

Members of Bourbon Women signing a barrel pick. (Photo by Bourbon Women)

13 | BOURBON WOMEN COCKTAILS FROM ACROSS THE COUNTRY

Smoked Chocolate-Bacon Manhattan

This easy riff on the Manhattan is a little bit breakfast and a little bit dessert. The layer of smoke (achieved with a cocktail smoker) charges up the bacon flavor.

2 ounces New Riff rye

1 ounce sweet vermouth

1–2 dashes orange bitters

1–2 dashes chocolate bitters

Half slice crispy bacon

Combine rye, vermouth, and bitters in a mixing glass and add ice. Stir until chilled. Strain into a chilled rocks or coupe glass. Place the bacon in the glass and smoke the cocktail.

Northern Kentucky branch of Bourbon Women—
submitted by Amy Bloomhuff

Kentucky isn't the only place you'll find bourbon drinkers (although there are a lot of us here). Sit at a serious whiskey bar anywhere in the country, and you're likely to spot patrons enjoying a fine pour or experimenting with a flight of bourbons. There are enthusiasts in every state who enjoy their whiskey and like to debate the finer points of the amber liquid in their glasses. Many of these people are women—strong-minded, independent women who know what they like.

When they travel, bourbon drinkers are likely to return home with suitcases full of craft bourbons and whiskeys from the small local distilleries they explored along the way. Like me, they probably google "distilleries near me" anytime they travel, and they have mastered the art of packing bottles safely in suitcases for the drive or flight home.

As the Bourbon Women organization expanded outside of its original home base in the Bluegrass region of Kentucky, it discovered like-minded women everywhere. To celebrate those adventurous, spirited drinkers from across the country, I've collected a bevy of cocktails from Bourbon Women branches nationwide. Many of these cocktails use local whiskeys or other local ingredients to create variations on the classics or to make small tweaks that connect the cocktail with the locality.

Here's what Peggy Noe Stevens, founder of Bourbon Women, has to say about the creation of the group's branches:

> When Bourbon Women first began, we were focused on the idea of Kentucky being the foundation to entertaining and educating women across our Bluegrass State. I had started my own company, PNSA, in 2008 and founded BW in 2011. As most women do, I was juggling a new company and a new association while simultaneously traveling back and forth to Indiana, balancing my son Utah's figure skating career as he trained in Indianapolis. I was determined to build business development for myself in that area.

> Along the way, the universe spoke and I met a dynamic Indiana woman named Natalie Clayton, who asked me to do a bourbon tasting for a museum she worked for, and I was delighted to oblige. Well, folks, that was it. The enthusiasm she had as well as the number of women who gravitated to me wanting to understand bourbon and asking repeatedly when we planned to begin a BW "chapter" in their area truly struck me. Bourbon Women needed to be beyond the borders of Kentucky, and we needed a bigger vision to reach women across the US. Indianapolis was our first "branch" (named after bourbon and branch water), and so it goes. Natalie became our first branch ambassador.

> We began receiving requests from cities across the US, and today we have women in virtually every state who are members and have over a dozen official branches to spread the great gospel of bourbon. Natalie, who I met in her twenties, has become a successful businesswoman in her own right and continues to be deeply engaged in BW and a dear friend. That is what BW does: we build relationships over a glass of bourbon and treasure long-lasting friendships. What a privilege and a duty all wrapped into one sensational journey.

Cocktail recipes submitted by Bourbon Women branches appear throughout this book, but this chapter is dedicated to those branches, their partners, and their creativity.

Sweet Corn–Cherry Whiskey Sour

Indianapolis branch of Bourbon Women—submitted by Samantha Mullennax

According to Sam, the Indianapolis branch ambassador, "Old 55 bourbon is as 'Indiana' and 'Midwest' as it gets. It is one of the few true 'field to bottle' distilleries in the world. Every grain used is sourced from the family farm. Its 100 percent sweet corn bourbon is unique, and sweet corn is very big here in Indiana." Likewise, "Hotel Tango is a local distillery in Indianapolis with a great story. Wilks and Wilson is another great Indianapolis company that makes elixirs, bitters, and simple syrups." With all these connections to the Hoosier State, this is a great cocktail for midwesterners.

2 ounces Old 55 sweet corn bourbon

½ ounce Hotel Tango cherry liqueur

¾ ounce lemon juice

½ ounce simple syrup

2–3 dashes Wilks and Wilson orange bitters

Garnish: lemon wheel, cocktail cherry

Combine ingredients in a shaking tin. Add ice and shake 10–12 seconds. Strain into a rocks glass with one large ice cube. Garnish.

Southern Star Queen Bee Cocktail

North Carolina branch of Bourbon Women—submitted by Vienna Barger

Delight your taste buds with this cocktail made from the Southern Star Distilling Company's products. It will warm even the frostiest toes.

2½ ounces Southern Star double-shot coffee bourbon cream liqueur

1 ounce Southern Star standard high-rye straight bourbon whiskey

½ ounce Carolina wildflower or sourwood honey

Garnish: freshly grated nutmeg

Combine ingredients in a shaker. Fill with ice and shake. Strain into an ice-filled rocks glass. Top with a dusting of freshly grated nutmeg.

Kentucky Buck

California branch of Bourbon Women—submitted by Erick Castro

This soda-topped bourbon buck from Erick Castro of Polite Provisions, San Diego, is a combination of spicy and sweet, with a fresh muddled strawberry for tartness. This somewhat unlikely combination works because the bourbon ties everything together with sweet notes of vanilla and fruit.

1 strawberry

¾ ounce ginger syrup (recipe follows)

2 ounces bourbon

¾ ounce lemon juice

2 dashes Angostura bitters

Club soda to top

Garnish: lemon wheel

In a cocktail shaker, muddle strawberry with ginger syrup. Add bourbon, lemon juice, and bitters. Add ice and shake until chilled. Double-strain into a Collins glass over ice and top with club soda. Garnish.

Ginger Syrup

Combine 3 parts sugar to 4 parts fresh ginger juice. Adjust the amount of ginger up or down, depending on the level of heat desired.

Hell or Hye Water

Texas branch of Bourbon Women—submitted by Hope Parkerson

This variation on a hurricane, from Hope Parkerson of Garrison Brothers Distillery, will leave sippers feeling refreshed and ready for more. It has a tiki vibe, with its tropical fruit flavors, but that bourbon kick moves the cocktail from Polynesia to Texas.

2 ounces Garrison Brothers bourbon

1 ounce pineapple juice

½ ounce passionfruit syrup

½ ounce fresh lime juice

1 dash lavender bitters

Garnish: lemon wheel, pineapple leaf

Shake ingredients with ice. Strain into an ice-filled rocks glass. Garnish.

Kentucky Buck.

Watermelon-Basil Moonshine Punch

New York branch of Bourbon Women—submitted by Kings County Distillery

Watermelon and basil punch? Yes, please! Mix up this moonshine punch for a thirst-quenching cocktail—but be careful, it also packs a punch. It's made with moonshine distilled in Kings County, New York.

2 ounces Kings County Distillery moonshine

¾ ounce fresh watermelon juice

½ ounce fresh lime juice

½ ounce basil syrup (recipe to right)

½ ounce Forthave Red Aperitivo

Club soda to top

Garnish: basil leaf

Combine ingredients (except club soda) in a tin, shake to combine, and chill. Double-strain over ice into a highball glass. Top with a splash of club soda. Garnish.

Basil Syrup

1 cup fresh basil leaves (packed)

1 cup water

1 cup white sugar

Bring water and sugar to a low boil and stir occasionally to combine. Once sugar is completely dissolved, reduce heat. Add basil leaves, pressing down to submerge. Simmer for 15 minutes. Remove from heat and strain through a chinois. Cool before use. Keeps 1 week in the fridge.

Head in the Clouds

Chicago branch of Bourbon Women—submitted by Adina Ewaldz

According to Adina: "The bourbon I used is from the distillery of chapter member Liz Henry. J. Henry 5-year bourbon is a four-grain expression from southern Wisconsin that works wonderfully in this drink. The Amer Picon used in this recipe comes from Golden Moon Distillery in Colorado. The northern Illinois–southern Wisconsin area was settled by many of Scandinavian descent, which explains the cloudberry jam. It's sold at Ikea, Whole Foods, and Amazon. The name of the drink was inspired by both these ingredients: the altitude of Colorado and the fact that cloudberries grow north of the Arctic Circle."

½ ounce lemon juice

½ ounce cinnamon simple syrup (recipe to right)

1 teaspoon cloudberry jam

2 ounces bourbon

½ ounce Amer Picon (or another bitter orange flavor)

3 dashes Peychaud's bitters

Garnish: orange peel or twist

Add ingredients to a cocktail shaker and fill with ice. Shake for 10–12 seconds. Double-strain into a chilled rocks or coupe glass and add garnish.

Cinnamon Simple Syrup

1 cup sugar

1 cup water

2 cinnamon sticks

Add ingredients to a small saucepan and heat until sugar dissolves. Cool completely before refrigerating. I store this syrup in the fridge with the cinnamon sticks in it.

Head in the Clouds.

Whicked Mary

Missouri branch of Bourbon Women—submitted by Jordan Germano

Whicked Pickle, a local hot pickle whiskey from Missouri, transforms a ho-hum Bloody Mary into a different beast entirely.

2 ounces Whicked Pickle whiskey

5 ounces Bloody Mary mix

Garnish: skewer of pickles and pepper

Combine ingredients in a pint glass over ice and garnish.

Campfire Old-Fashioned

Northern Kentucky branch of Bourbon Women—submitted by Amy Bloomhuff

Smoking simple syrup creates the same rich depth of flavor you'd get from smoking a glass, but the smoke doesn't disperse as the cocktail is poured. The two sweet bitters add complexity to contrast with the smoke. Top with a torched marshmallow (or three), and the Campfire Old-Fashioned is complete.

2 ounces New Riff Winter Whiskey bourbon

½ ounce smoked simple syrup (recipe follows)

1–2 dashes Woodford cherry bitters

1–2 dashes black walnut bitters

Garnish: Luxardo cherry, toasted marshmallow

Combine ingredients in a mixing glass. Add ice and stir until chilled. Strain into a rocks glass with ice and add garnish.

Smoked Simple Syrup

Place simple syrup in an open, smoker-safe container. After meat has finished smoking, place the container in the smoker and smoke for 30–60 minutes, or to taste.

Campfire Old-Fashioned.

Indy X Root Beer Float

Indianapolis branch of Bourbon Women—submitted by Samantha Mullennax

Sam, the branch ambassador, says, "Hotel Tango is a local company in Indianapolis, and Triple X is a famous root beer from Lafayette, Indiana, where Purdue University is located. It's one of those bucket list things. Everyone here has heard about Triple X or knows about it." Adding a healthy helping of vanilla ice cream results in an adult version of a childhood classic. Just be sure to serve this one with a spoon to get every last drop. I took the initiative and added a little whipped cream and mint to mine and served it in a goblet to make a full dessert in a glass.

3–4 ounces Triple X root beer

2 ounces Hotel Tango bourbon

½ ounce Hotel Tango cherry liqueur

2 scoops vanilla ice cream

Garnish: cherry

Add chilled root beer, bourbon, and liqueur to the bottom of a highball glass. Add ice cream and another splash of root beer. Top with a cherry and serve with a spoon.

Michigan I-75

Michigan branch of Bourbon Women—submitted by Jeri Seeley

Michiganders know all about the I-75, and this fancy sour is a great twist combining a French 75 (gin sour topped with bubbles) and a Fitzgerald (gin sour served on the rocks). Combining them results in a bourbon cocktail with a punch like the traffic on the I-75. Use Detroit City Distillery bourbon to get the full effect of a Michigan classic. I love the contrast between the sweet bubbles of the prosecco and the tart whiskey sour underneath.

2 ounces Detroit City Distillery bourbon (or any local bourbon)

¾ ounce simple syrup

¾ ounce fresh squeezed and strained lemon juice

2 dashes Angostura bitters

1 ounce chilled prosecco or Brut champagne

Garnish: lemon twist

In a shaker tin filled with ice, add bourbon, simple syrup, lemon juice, and bitters. Shake well. Strain into a champagne or coupe glass. Top with chilled prosecco or champagne and garnish.

Michigan I-75.

That's My Peach

Atlanta branch of Bourbon Women—submitted by Joanna Pruett

This peachy sour highlights the unique products Georgia has to offer. Garnishing the cocktail with a fresh Georgia peach in the height of summer makes it that much sweeter. Let the peach slice and candied ginger infuse in the cocktail as you sip it and eat them last as the dessert to your cocktail.

1½ ounces ASW bourbon

1 ounce Blended Family No. 4 peach liqueur

½ ounce fresh lemon juice

½ ounce simple syrup

Club soda to top

Garnish: fresh peach slice, candied ginger

Combine bourbon, peach liqueur, lemon juice, and simple syrup in a shaker tin. Add ice and shake briskly for about 20 seconds. Strain over fresh ice in a highball glass. Top with club soda for extra pizzazz. Garnish.

Tennessee Takes Manhattan

Tennessee branch of Bourbon Women—submitted by April Cantrell

This take on a Perfect Manhattan highlights the smooth tones of Tennessee whiskey. The bitter herbal notes of Benedictine balance the dry vermouth, and the extra orange from the bitters ties both the liqueur and the vermouth to the Tennessee whiskey.

1½ ounces Tennessee whiskey or bourbon (Leiper's Fork Distillery bottled in bond Tennessee whiskey or Old Dominick's Huling Station bourbon is recommended)

½ ounce Benedictine

½ ounce dry vermouth

4–5 dashes orange bitters

Garnish: Luxardo cherry

Combine ingredients in a mixing cup filled with ice. Stir vigorously for at least 30 seconds. Strain into a chilled cocktail glass and garnish.

KCD Margarita

New York branch of Bourbon Women—submitted by Kings County Distillery

This margarita may not use bourbon, but the tarty heat of the grapefruit-jalapeño moonshine gives it a real kick.

2 ounces Kings County Distillery grapefruit-jalapeño moonshine

1 ounce fresh lime juice

¾ ounce simple syrup

Garnish: lime wheel

Combine ingredients in a tin with ice and shake well to combine and chill. Strain into a salt-rimmed rocks glass over fresh ice. Garnish.

Mango Bourbon Mule

Northern Kentucky branch of Bourbon Women—submitted by Amy Bloomhuff

When it's summertime and you want a light cocktail that's easy to put together, this one is perfect. It has just three ingredients and can be built right in the copper mule mug. The most time-consuming element is peeling and cutting the fresh mango for garnish.

1–2 ounces Reàl Cocktail Ingredients mango syrup

1½–2 ounces bourbon

Ginger beer or ginger ale

Garnish: fresh mint sprig and/ or fresh mango slice

Add mango syrup and bourbon to a copper mule mug. Give it a quick swirl, fill with ice, and top with ginger beer or ginger ale. Garnish.

ACKNOWLEDGMENTS

There are so many people to thank. This book is a love song to all the Bourbon Women who sip, create, and experiment—inside the industry and out. Your love of bourbon and bourbon culture and your efforts to encourage others to drink more whiskey inspire me to create cocktails each day. Thank you to Susan Reigler and Peggy Noe Stevens for dropping this project in my lap by saying, "We think you should do this. This is perfect for you." Special thanks to Susan for her mentorship as I worked on my first book, including her encouragement, editorial suggestions, and insight. Peggy and Susan also graciously allowed me to publish my recipes that previously appeared in their books: from *Which Fork Do I Use with My Bourbon?* Fleur-de-Lis Manhattan, Dark Quarter, and Bold Old (renamed Kentucky Smolder here); from *More Kentucky Bourbon Cocktails* by Joy Perrine and Susan Reigler, the winning cocktail recipes from the "Not Your Pink Drink" contest from 2012 through 2015. Additional photography was provided by Chris Joyce KY, where noted.

Thanks to my husband, my family, and my best friend. My husband encouraged me while I grew our bourbon and spirits collection to amazing proportions and filled up our refrigerator with syrups, infusions, and experiments. He has spent years as my first taster, and I know that when he won't hand the cocktail back to me I'm on the right track.

Thanks to my parents and brother for their support and love while I worked on this book. Special thanks to both my best friend Kate and my mom (the original Bourbon Women posse) for their cocktail testing and tasting assistance over the last seven years as I delivered tiny bottles of cocktails to their kitchens and front stoops for sampling. Thanks to Dad for the boxes of vintage glassware dropped off on the back porch whenever he found great pieces.

Also, thanks to my early readers who helped shape the book with their suggestions: Kate Osborn, Christin Head, Laura Ellison, Beth Johnson, Angela Vann, and Andy Wibbels.

Finally, thank you to that amazing online community of mixologists, home bartenders, cocktail creators, and bourbon lovers. You all inspire my creations, my experiments, and my goal of finding a way to get whiskey into everyone's cocktails.

RESOURCES AND SUGGESTED READING

Arnold, Dave. *Liquid Intelligence: The Art and Science of the Perfect Cocktail.* New York: W. W. Norton, 2014.

Bitterman, Mark. *Bitterman's Field Guide to Bitters & Amari: 500 Bitters; 50 Amari; 123 Recipes for Cocktails, Food & Homemade Bitters.* Kansas City, MO: Andrews McMeel, 2015.

Carlton, Carla Harris. *Barrel Strength Bourbon: The Explosive Growth of America's Whiskey.* Birmingham, AL: Clerisy Press, 2017.

Day, Alex, Nick Fauchald, and David Kaplan. *Cocktail Codex: Fundamentals, Formulas, Evolutions.* Berkeley, CA: Ten Speed Press, 2018.

Day, Alex, Nick Fauchald and David Kaplan. *Death & Co: Modern Classic Cocktails.* Berkeley, CA: Ten Speed Press, 2014.

DeGroff, Dale. *The Craft of the Cocktail: Everything You Need to Know to Be a Master Bartender.* New York: Clarkson Potter, 2002.

Greene, Heather. *Whisk(e)y Distilled: A Populist Guide to the Water of Life.* New York: Avery, 2015.

Minnick, Fred. *Bourbon: The Rise, Fall, and Rebirth of an American Whiskey.* Minneapolis: Voyageur Press, 2016.

Morgenthaler, Jeffrey. *The Bar Book: Elements of Cocktail Technique.* San Francisco: Chronicle Books, 2014.

Page, Karen, and Andrew Dornenburg. *The Flavor Bible: The Essential Guide to Culinary Creativity, Based on the Wisdom of America's Most Imaginative Chefs.* New York: Little, Brown, 2008.

Perrine, Joy, and Susan Reigler. *The Kentucky Bourbon Cocktail Book.* Lexington: University Press of Kentucky, 2009.

Perrine, Joy, and Susan Reigler. *More Kentucky Bourbon Cocktails.* Lexington: University Press of Kentucky, 2016.

Reigler, Susan, and Michael Veach. *The Bourbon Tasting Notebook.* 2nd ed. Morley, MO: Acclaim Press, 2018.

Rogers, Adam. *Proof: The Science of Booze.* Boston: Mariner Books, 2015.

Simonson, Robert. *The Old Fashioned: The Story of the Word's First Classic Cocktail with Recipes and Lore.* Berkeley, CA: Ten Speed Press, 2014.

Stevens, Peggy Noe, and Susan Reigler. *Which Fork Do I Use with My Bourbon? Setting the Table for Tastings, Food Pairings, Dinners, and Cocktail Parties.* Lexington, KY: South Limestone Books, 2020.

Wondrich, David. *Imbibe! Updated and Revised Edition: From Absinthe Cocktail to Whiskey Smash, a Salute in Stories and Drinks to "Professor" Jerry Thomas, Pioneer of the American Bar.* New York: Perigee, 2015.

INDEX

29–31; infusions, 41, 48–49; syrups, 35. *See also specific fruits*

ABOUT THE AUTHOR

Heather Wibbels, an award-winning mixologist and chair of the Bourbon Women Board of Directors, is a digital content creator, writer, and photographer. As an executive bourbon steward, her goal is to turn the world into whiskey drinkers one cocktail at a time with her craft cocktail creations. She works with various brands and companies to develop cocktails and provide cocktail education to the home mixologist and bourbon enthusiast. For her most recent creations, visit **www.cocktailcontessa.com**. When she's not writing, making cocktails, or tasting whiskey, you can find her cycling through the Bluegrass State or fostering kittens.

ABOUT BOURBON WOMEN

Founded in 2011, Bourbon Women is *the* organization for those who are passionate about bourbon culture, women, and the promise of adventure when the two are combined. With branches across the United States, the organization has held more than 200 bourbon events and works closely with both heritage and craft distillers. Bourbon Women is a one-of-a-kind organization devoted to creating and fostering connections between women and the bourbon and spirits industry, and it embodies all the fun and meaningful things that can happen when women gather and share a glass of bourbon.

Bourbon Women maintains strong ties to the industry through partnerships with the Kentucky Distillers Association, Distilled Spirits Council of the United States (DISCUS), and local and nation-wide bourbon groups. In addition to connecting consumers to the bourbon industry, it facilitates relationships among its members who are involved in the bourbon, spirits, and hospitality industries.

By encouraging members' personal and professional development, as well as creating an environment to cultivate and inspire deep and meaningful relationships, Bourbon Women's goal is to empower members and foster a positive, inclusive, socially responsible environment for bourbon education and culture. Visit **www.bourbonwomen.org** for more information.